Adult Coloring Book

- Doodles -

Volume 1

I0487129

Brought to you by Kooky Book Lovers
A subsidiary of Kooky Puzzle Lovers
At
kookypuzzlelovers.com

Check out our website for more coloring books! It's under the section BOOKS at kookypuzzlelovers.com.

While you're on our site, check out the puzzles and personalized journals.

What is needed:

1. Markers, colored pencils, crayons, or paint.
2. Wax Paper. (Prevents bleed-thru)
3. If in doubt check out our website for examples.
4. Grab a coffee, tea, or your favorite beverage.
5. Turn on your favorite music.
6. Take a deep breath.
7. Begin.
8. Send kookypuzzlelovers.com your finished product so we can display it!

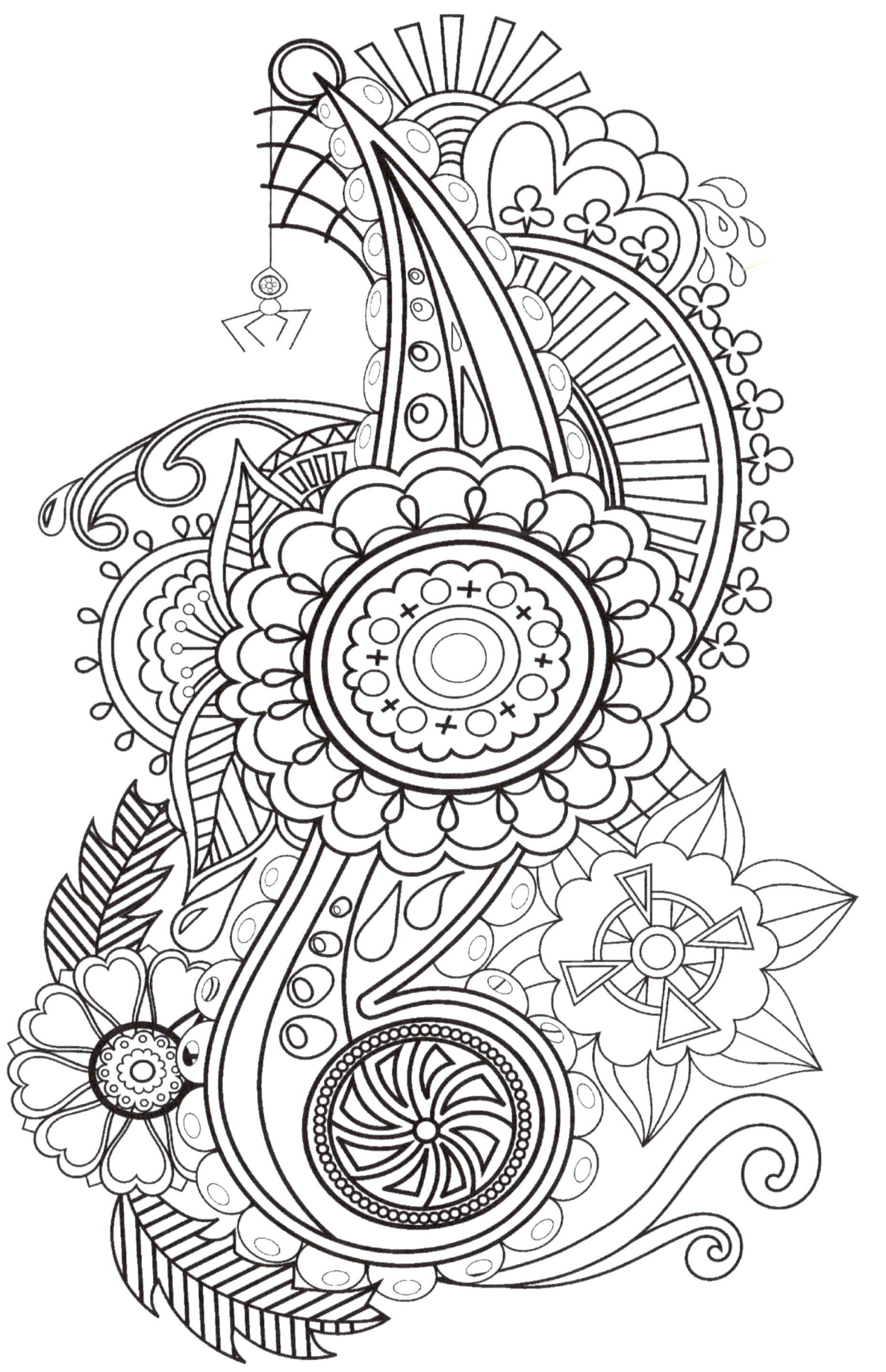

Insert Wax Paper Here

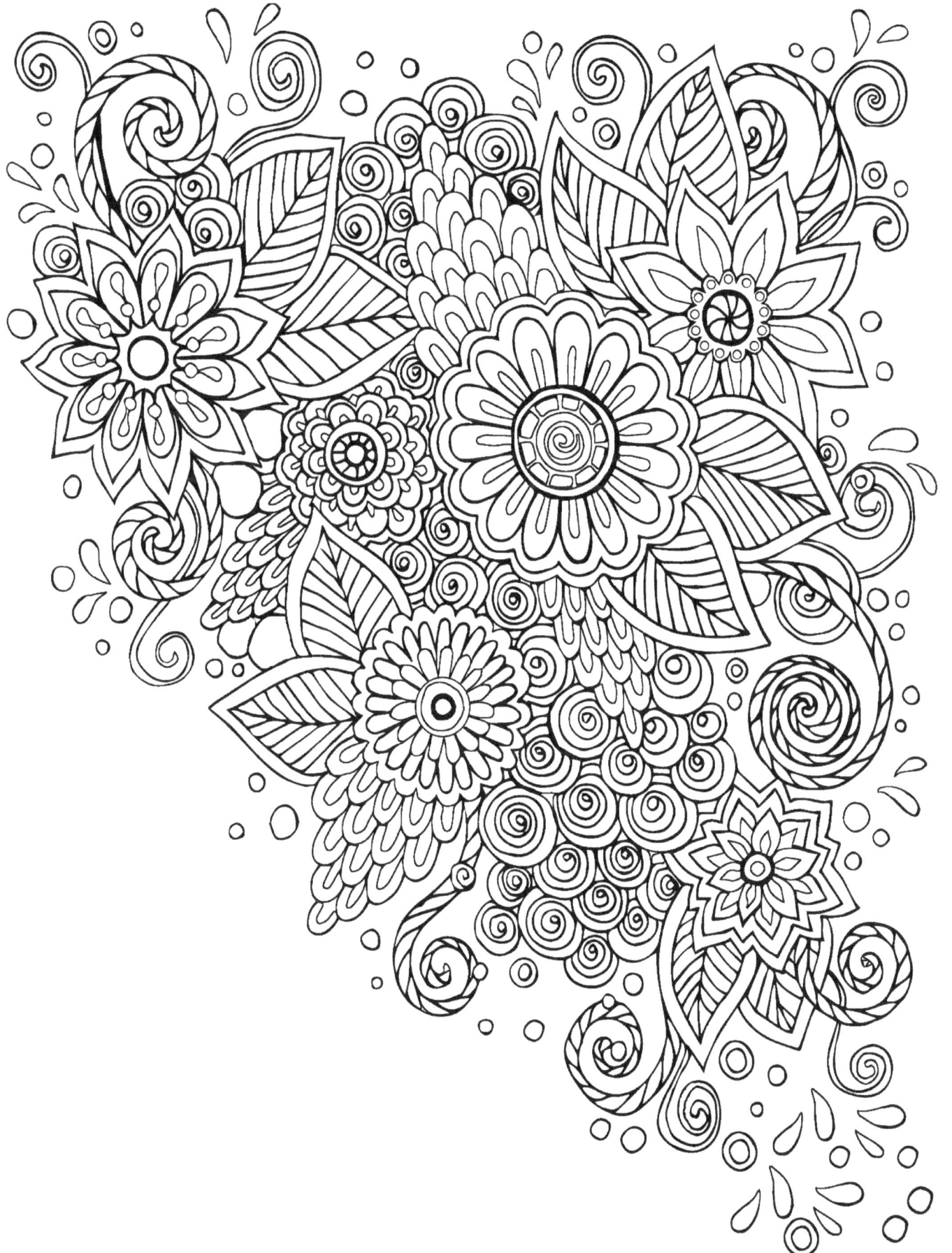

Insert Wax Paper Here

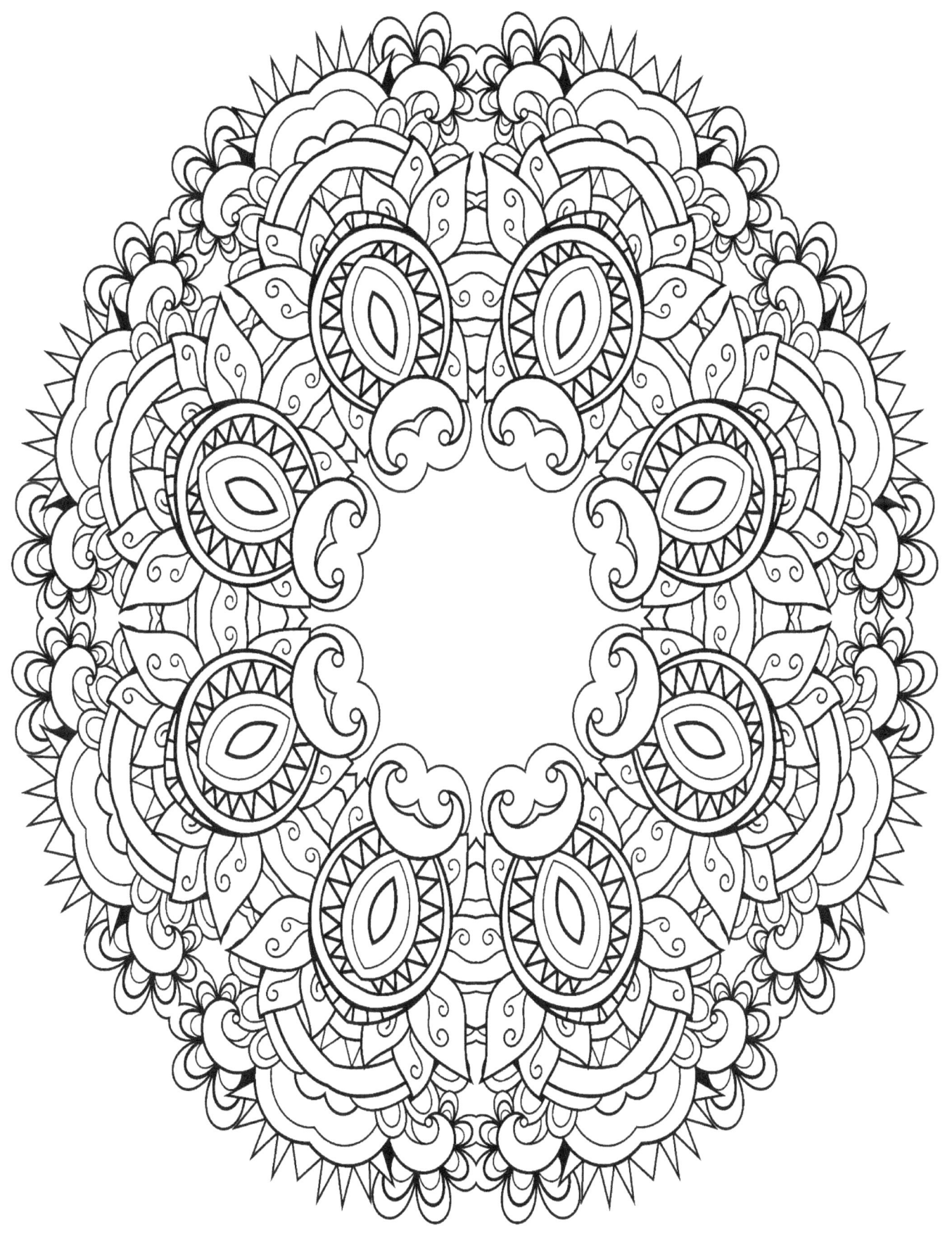

Insert Wax Paper Here

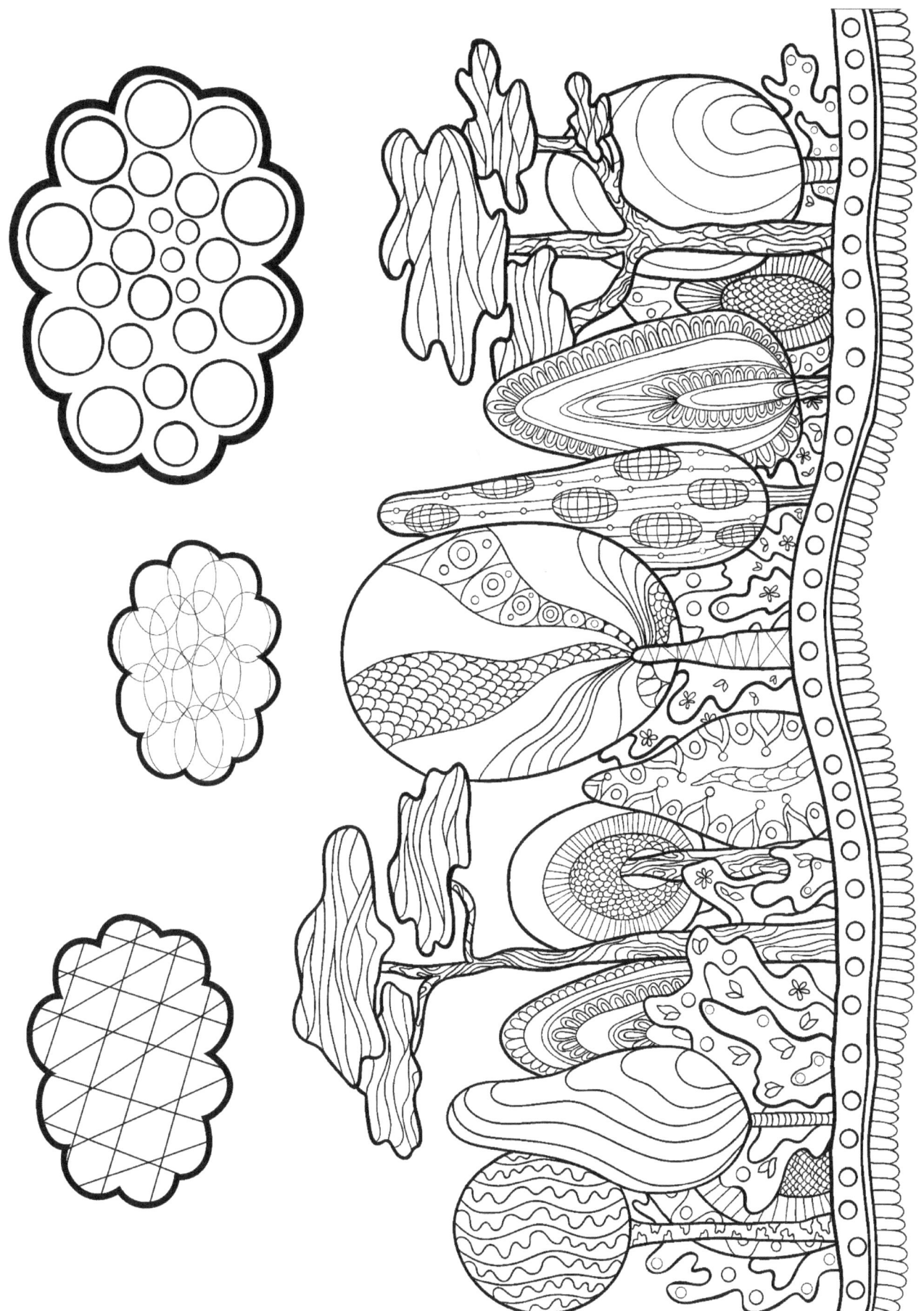

Insert Wax Paper Here

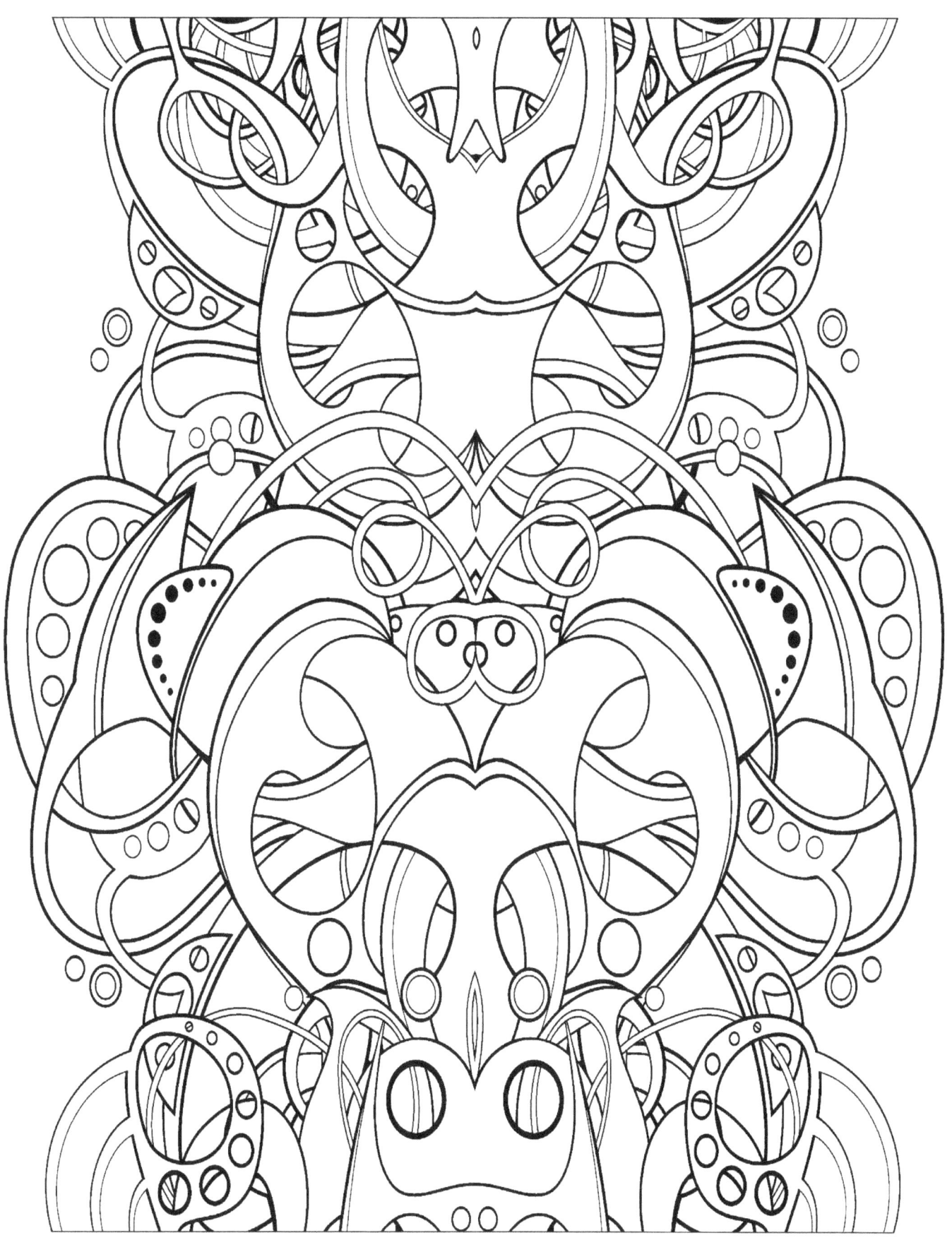

Insert Wax Paper Here

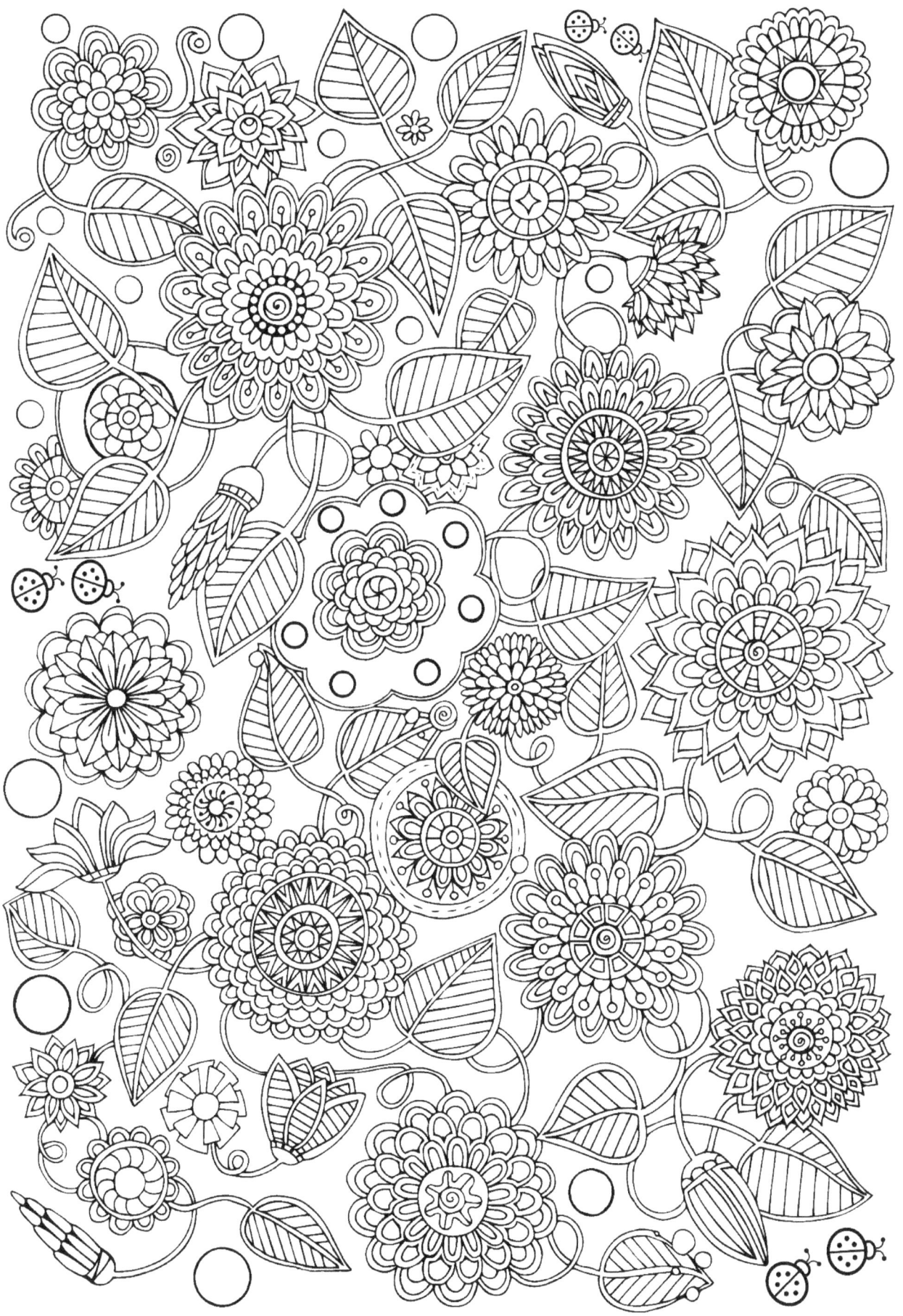

Insert Wax Paper Here

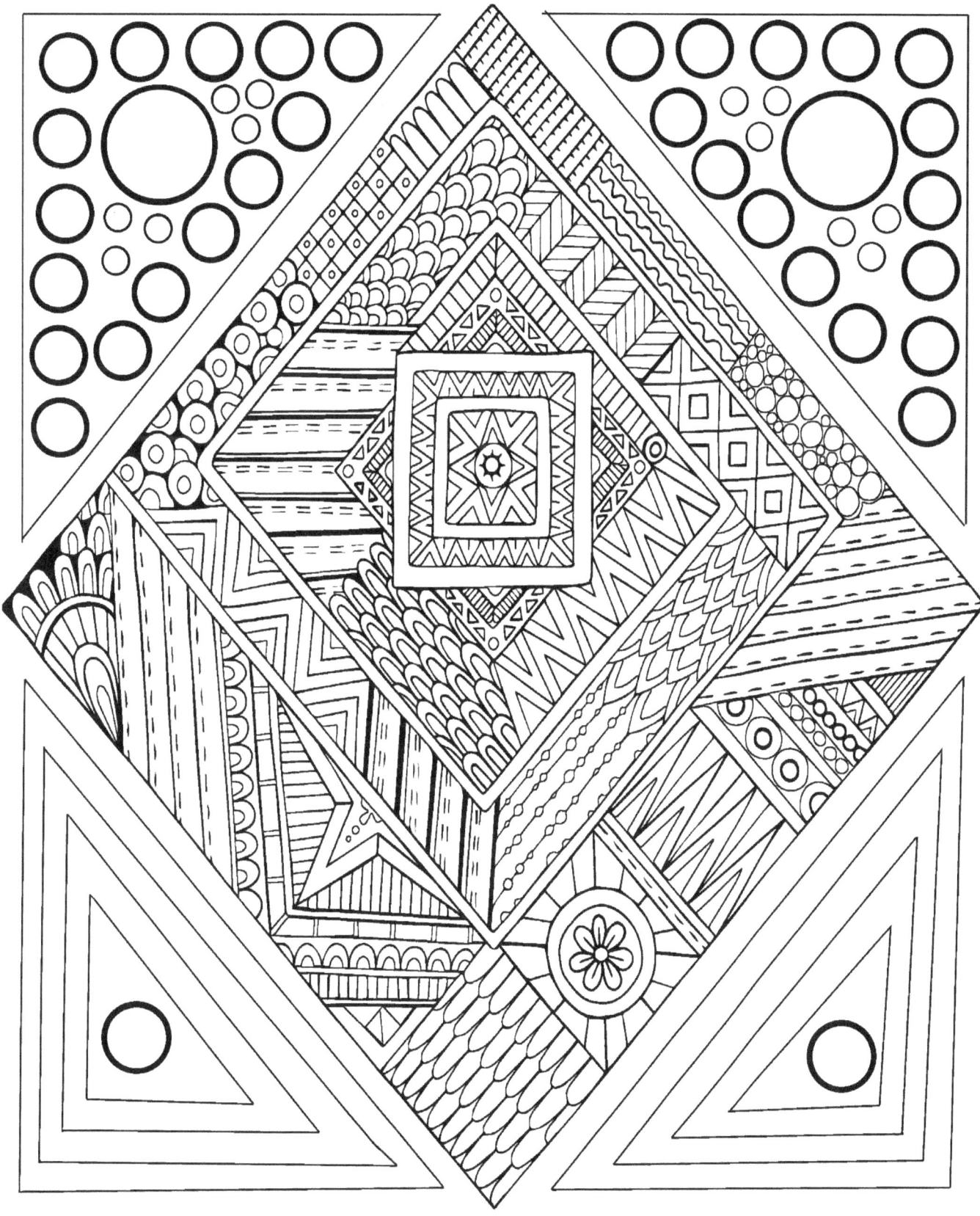

Insert Wax Paper Here

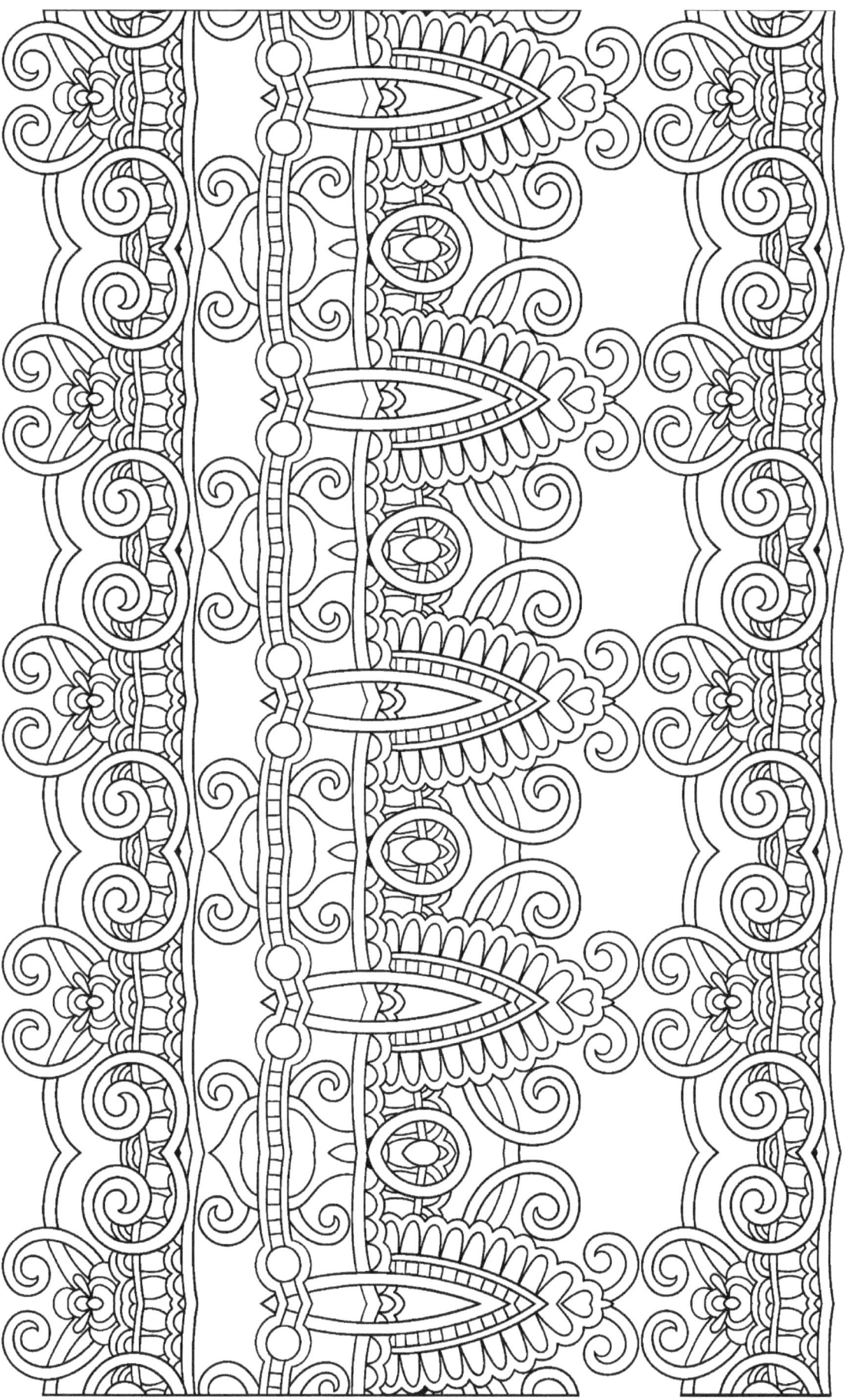

Insert Wax Paper Here

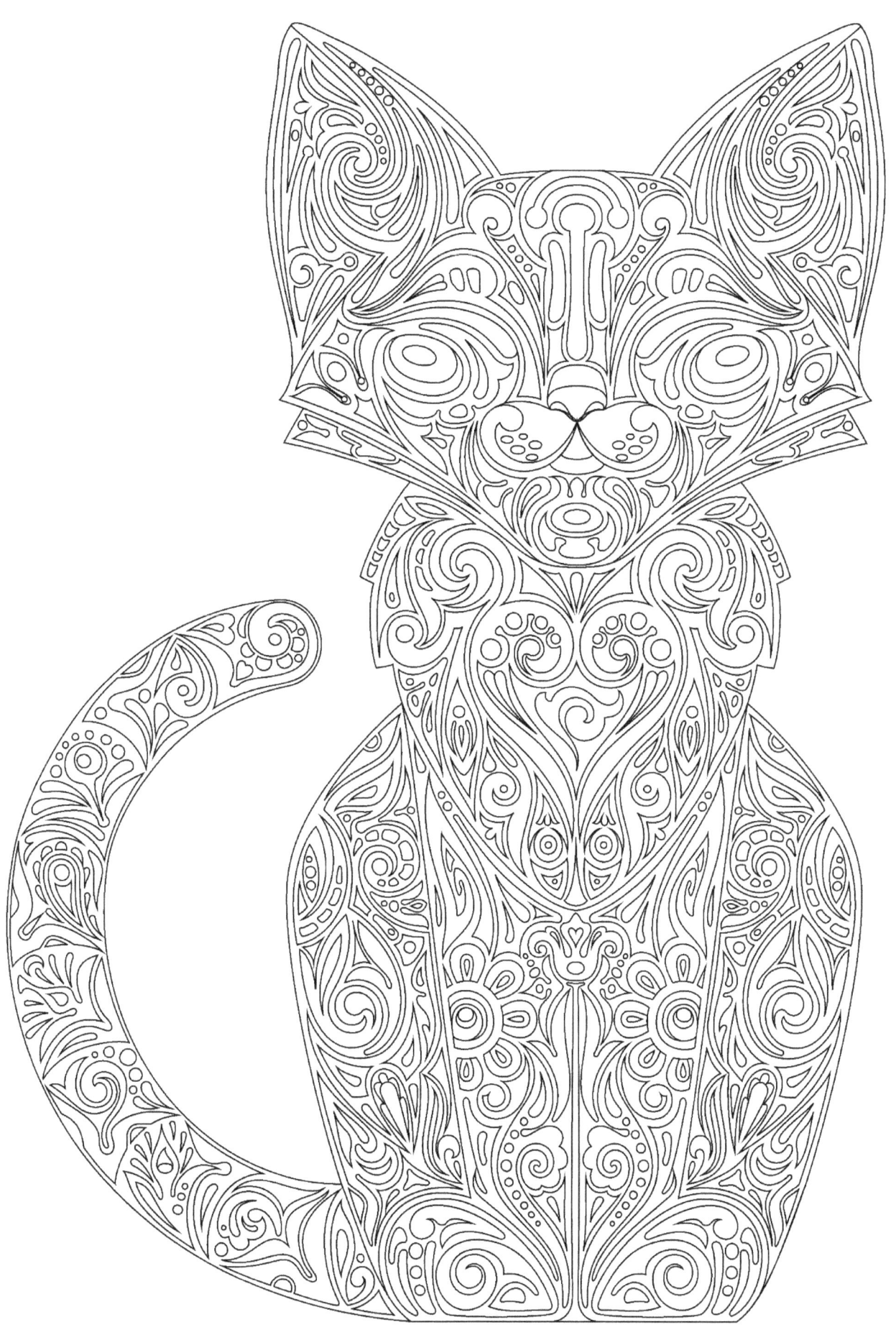

Insert Wax Paper Here

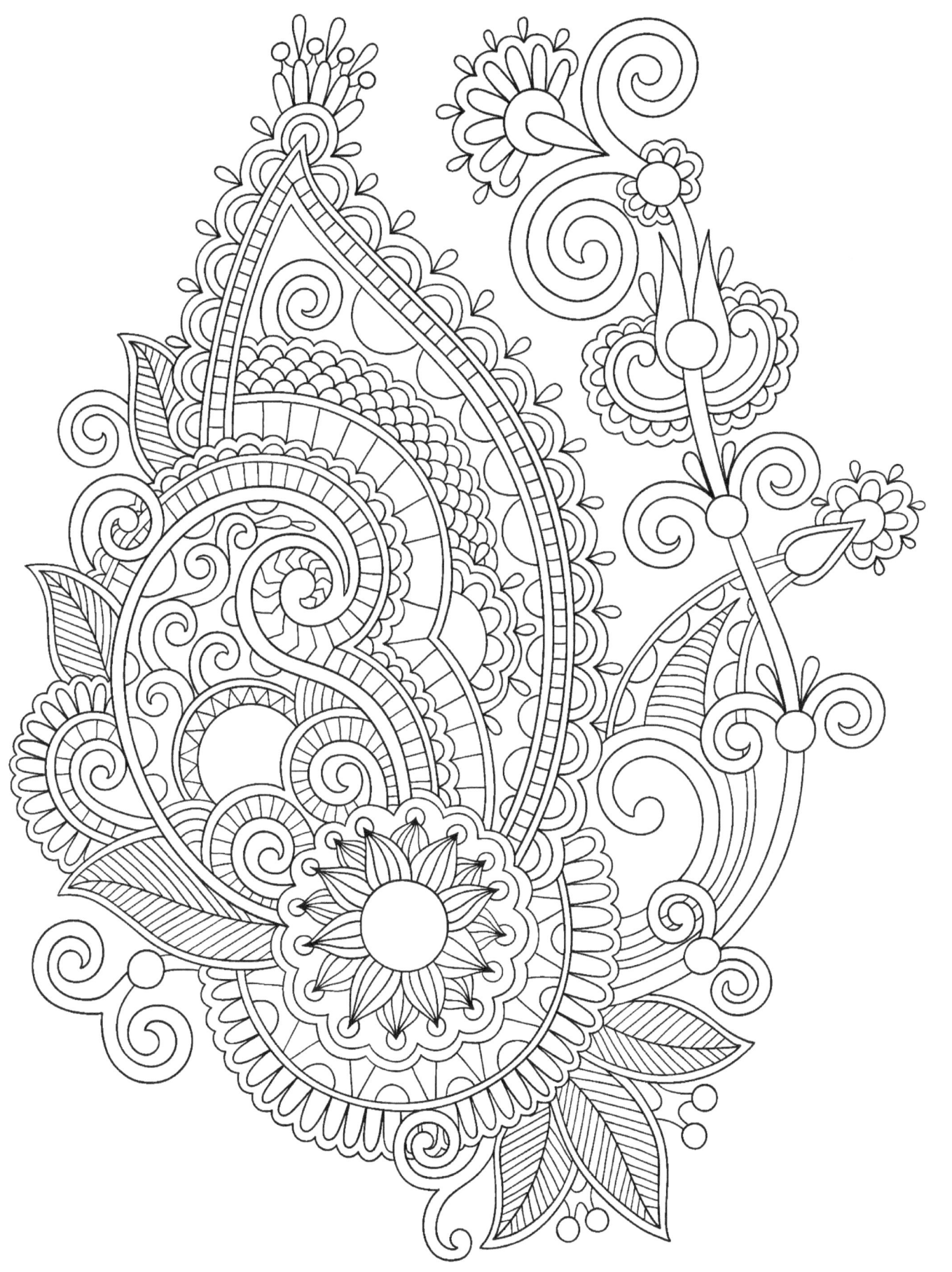

Insert Wax Paper Here

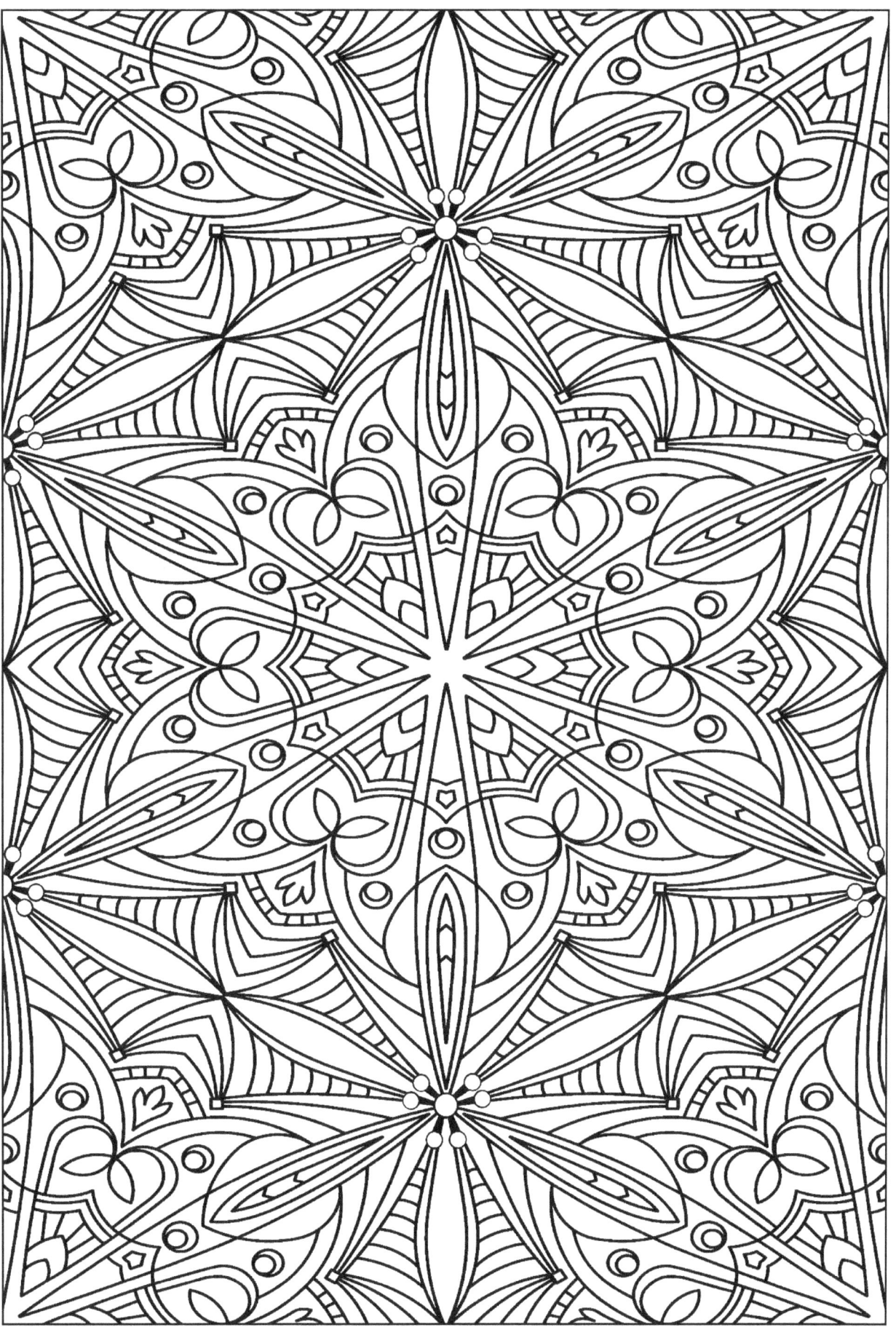

Insert Wax Paper Here

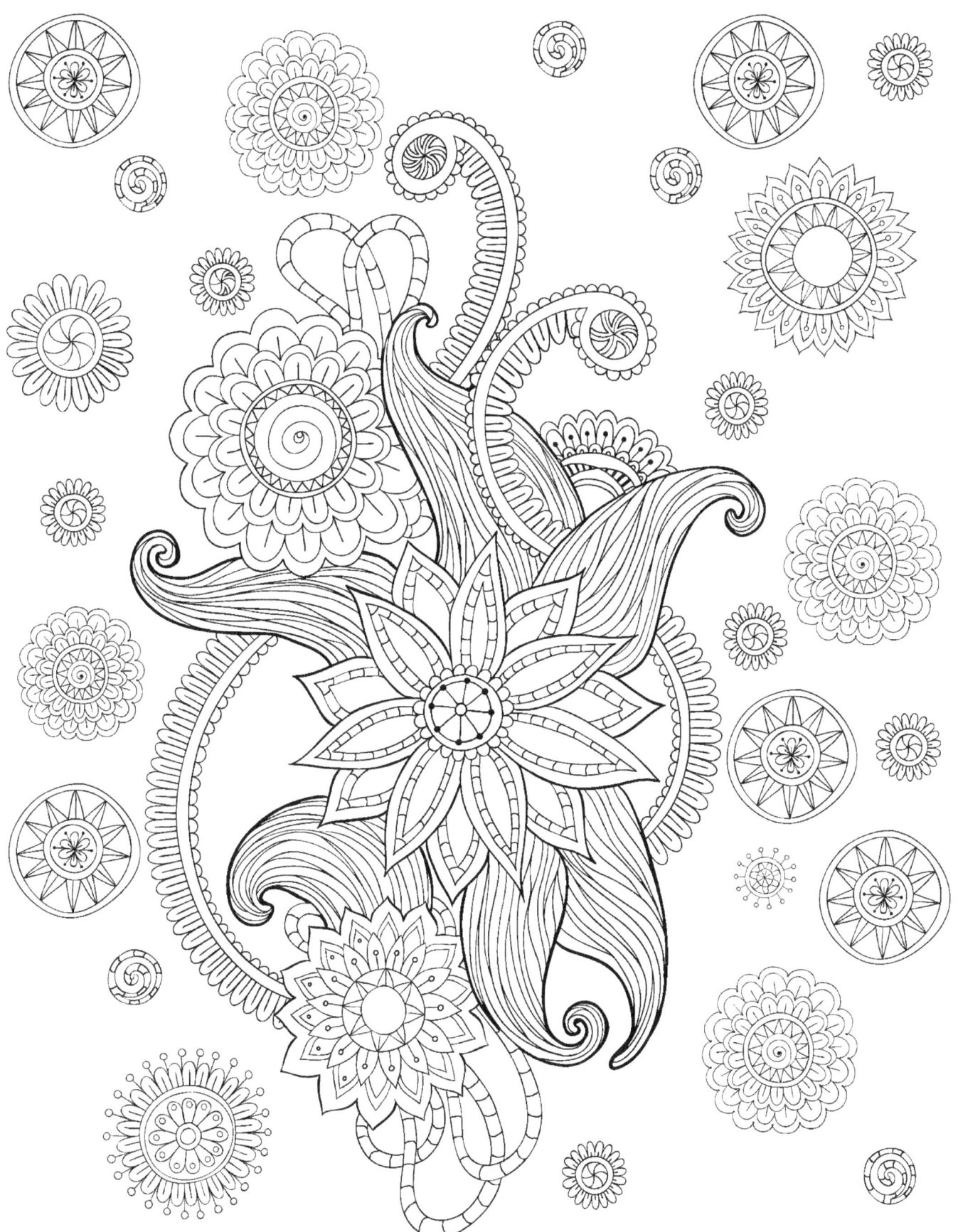

Insert Wax Paper Here

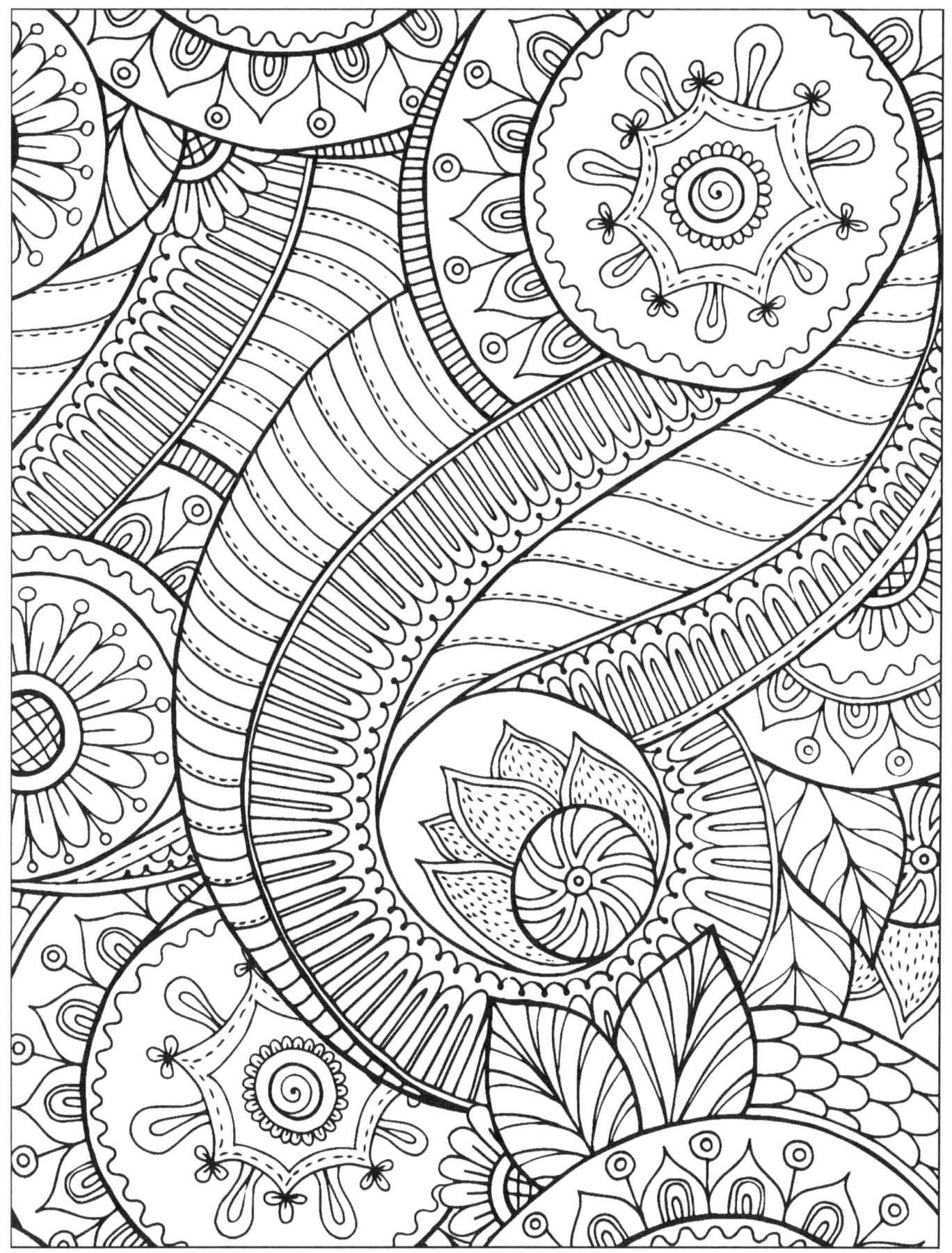

Insert Wax Paper Here

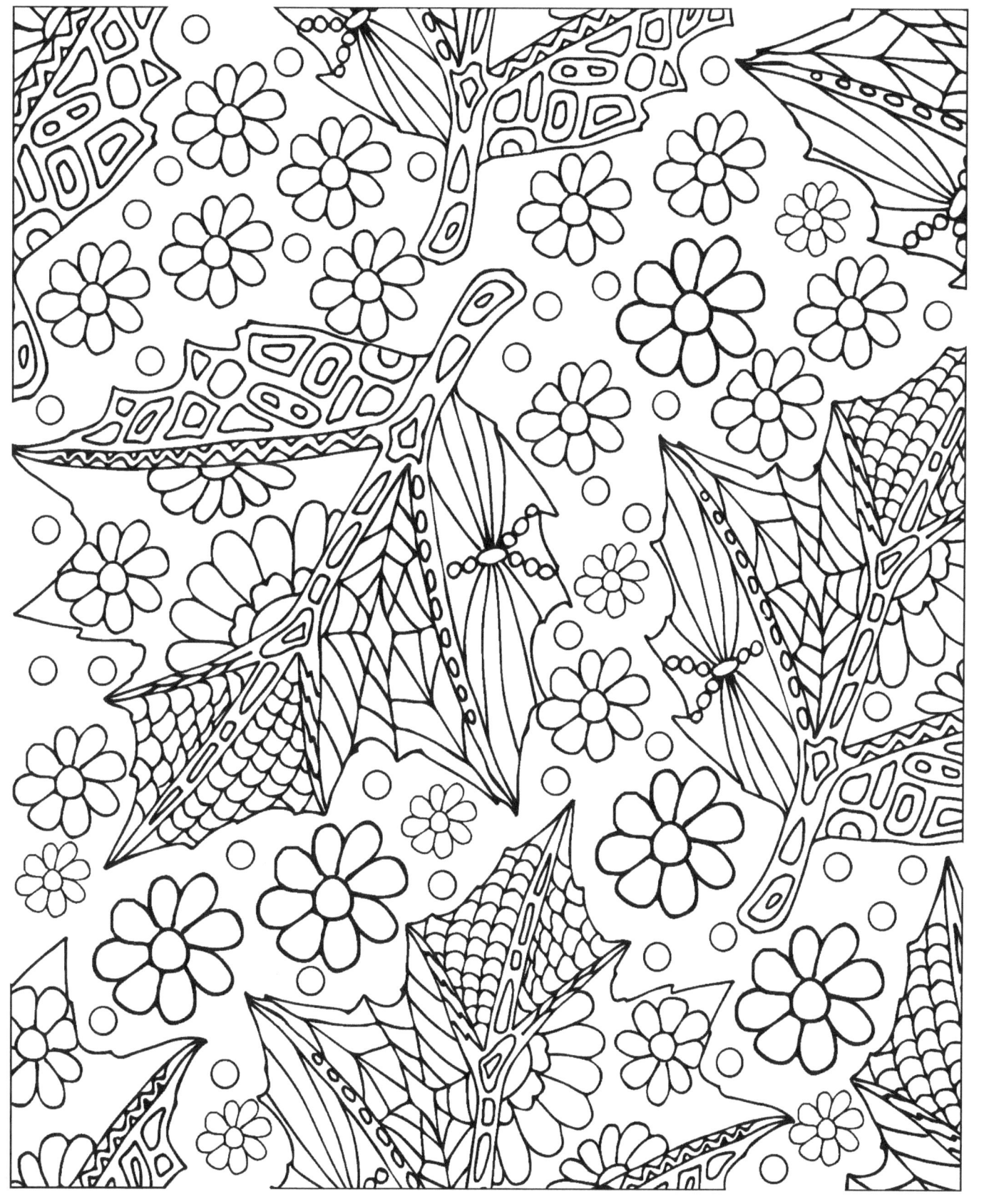

Insert Wax Paper Here

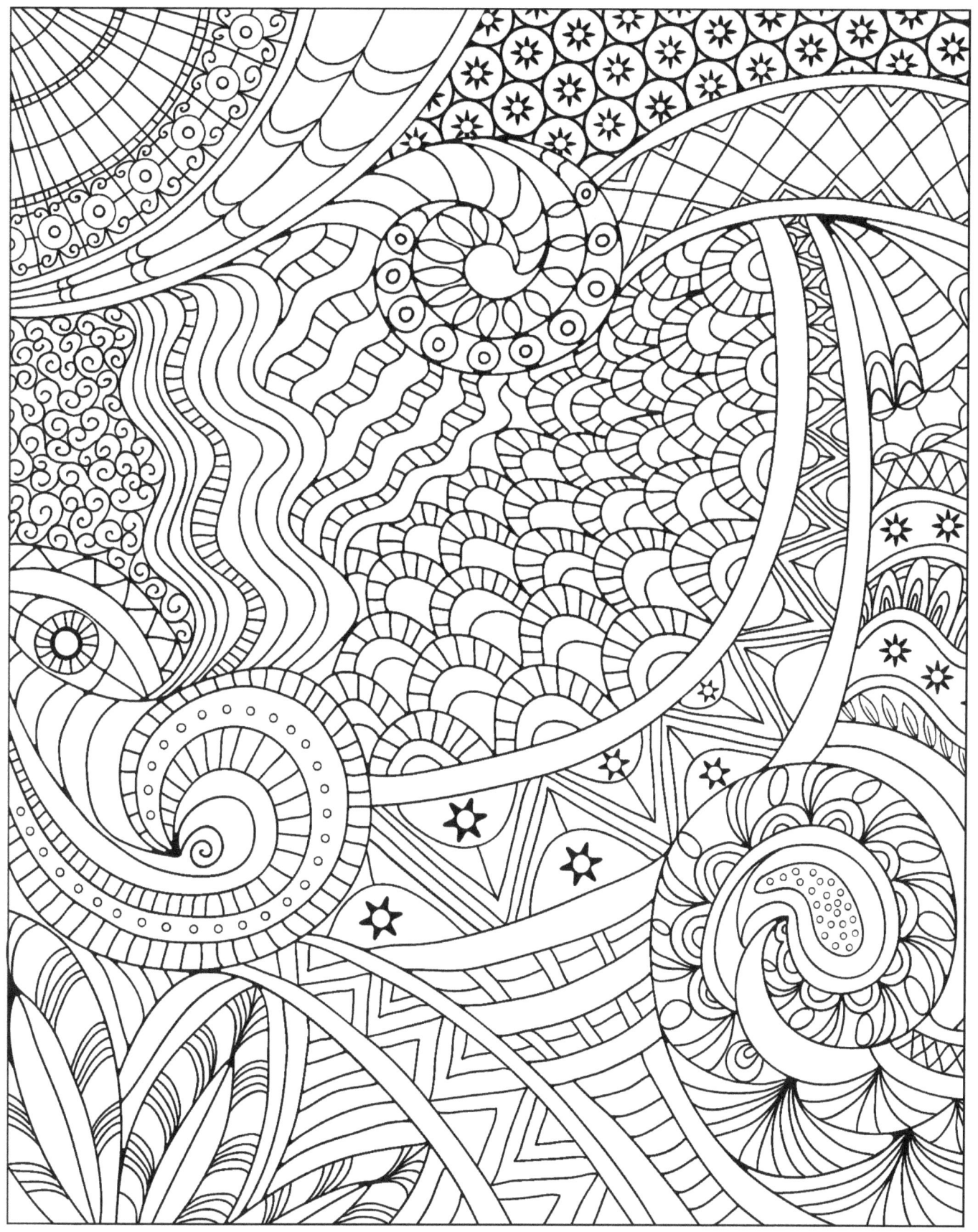

Insert Wax Paper Here

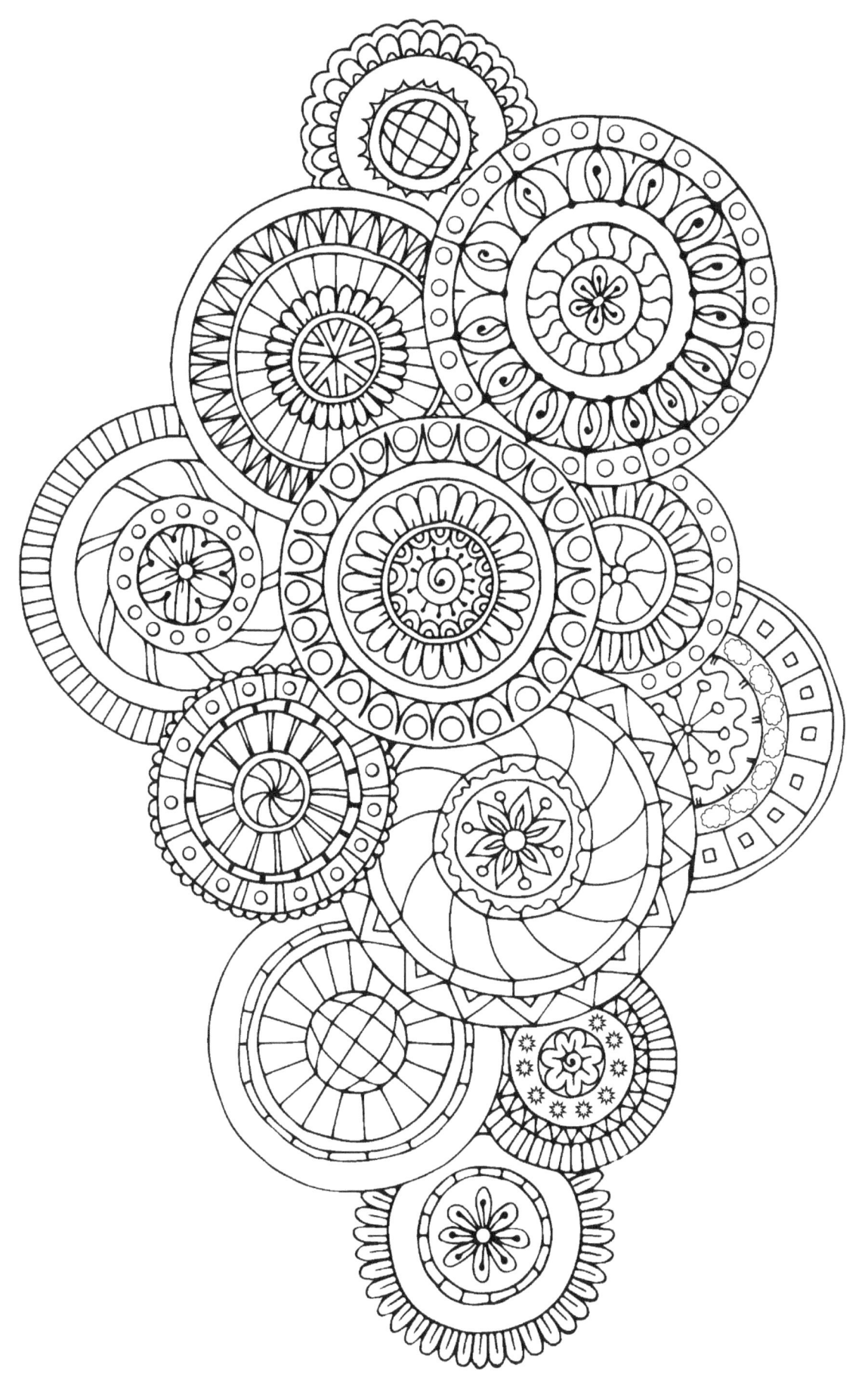

Insert Wax Paper Here

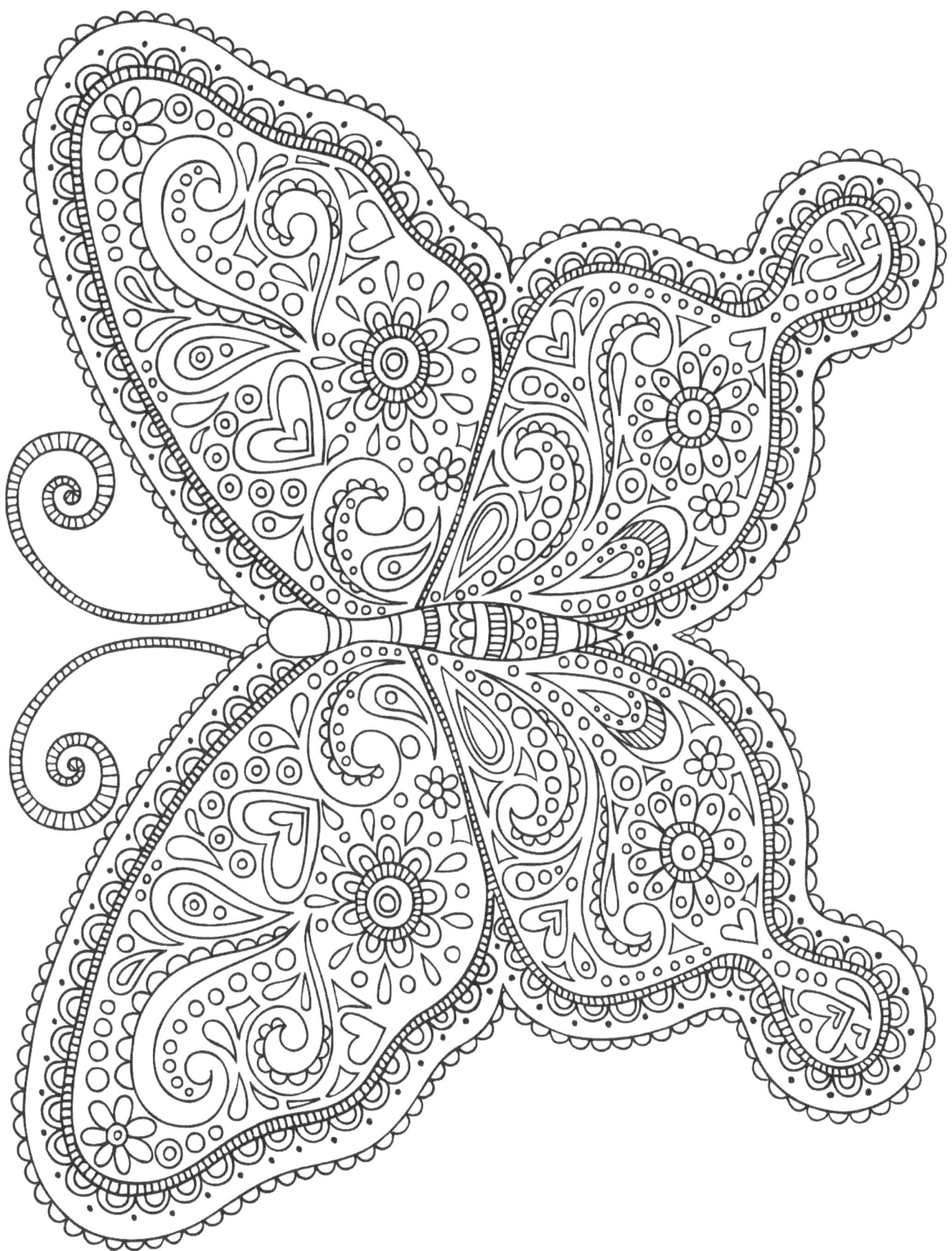

Insert Wax Paper Here

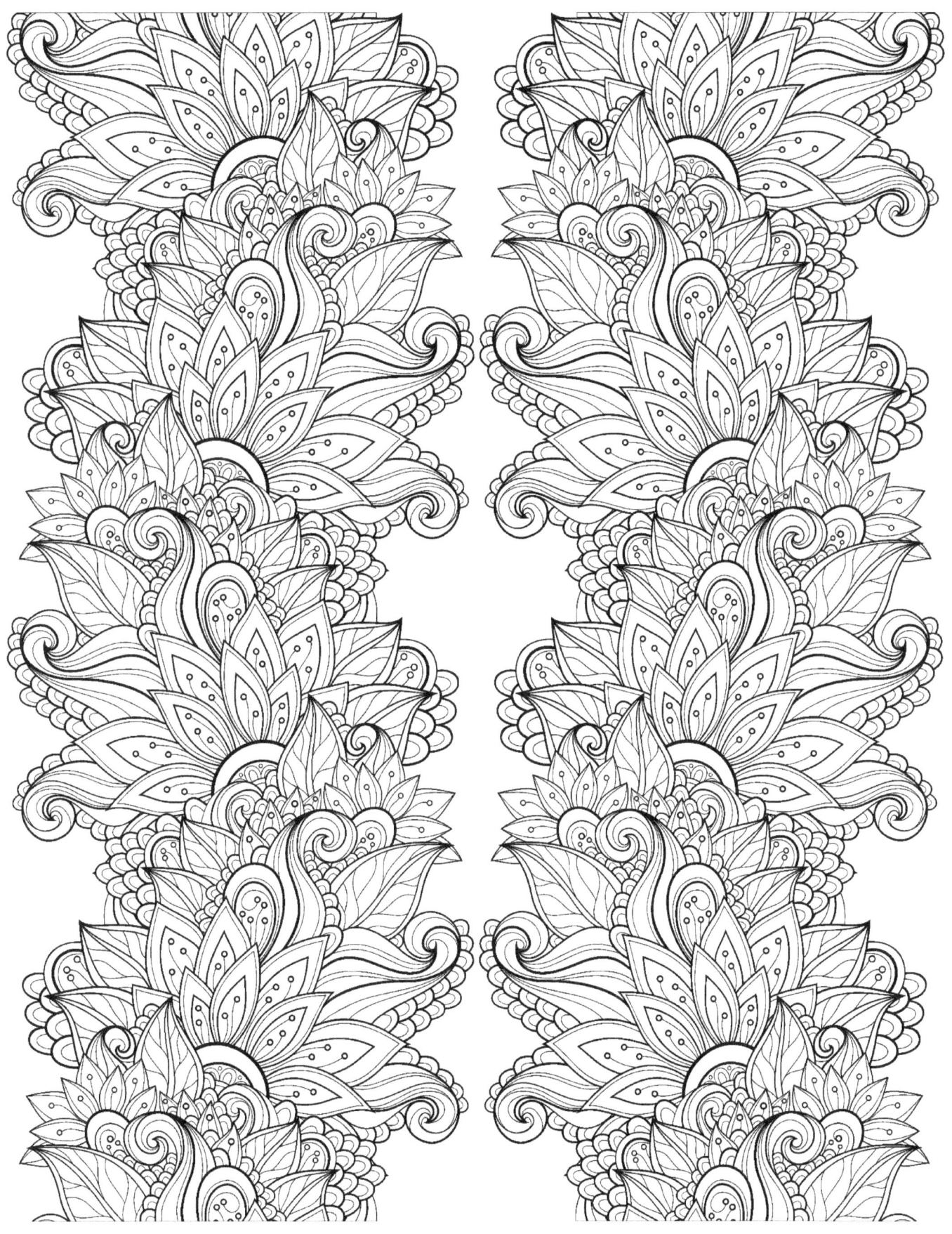

Insert Wax Paper Here

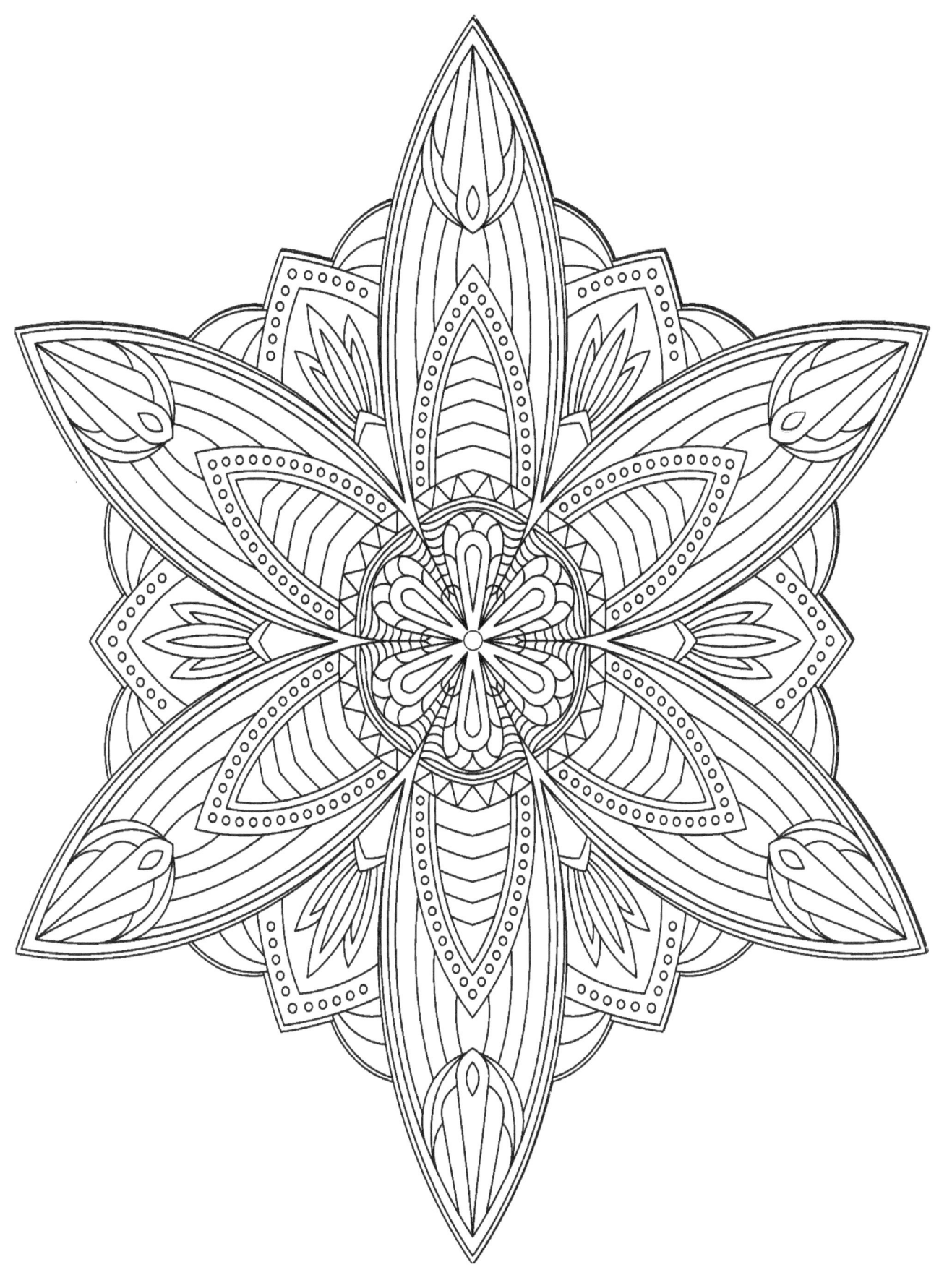

Insert Wax Paper Here

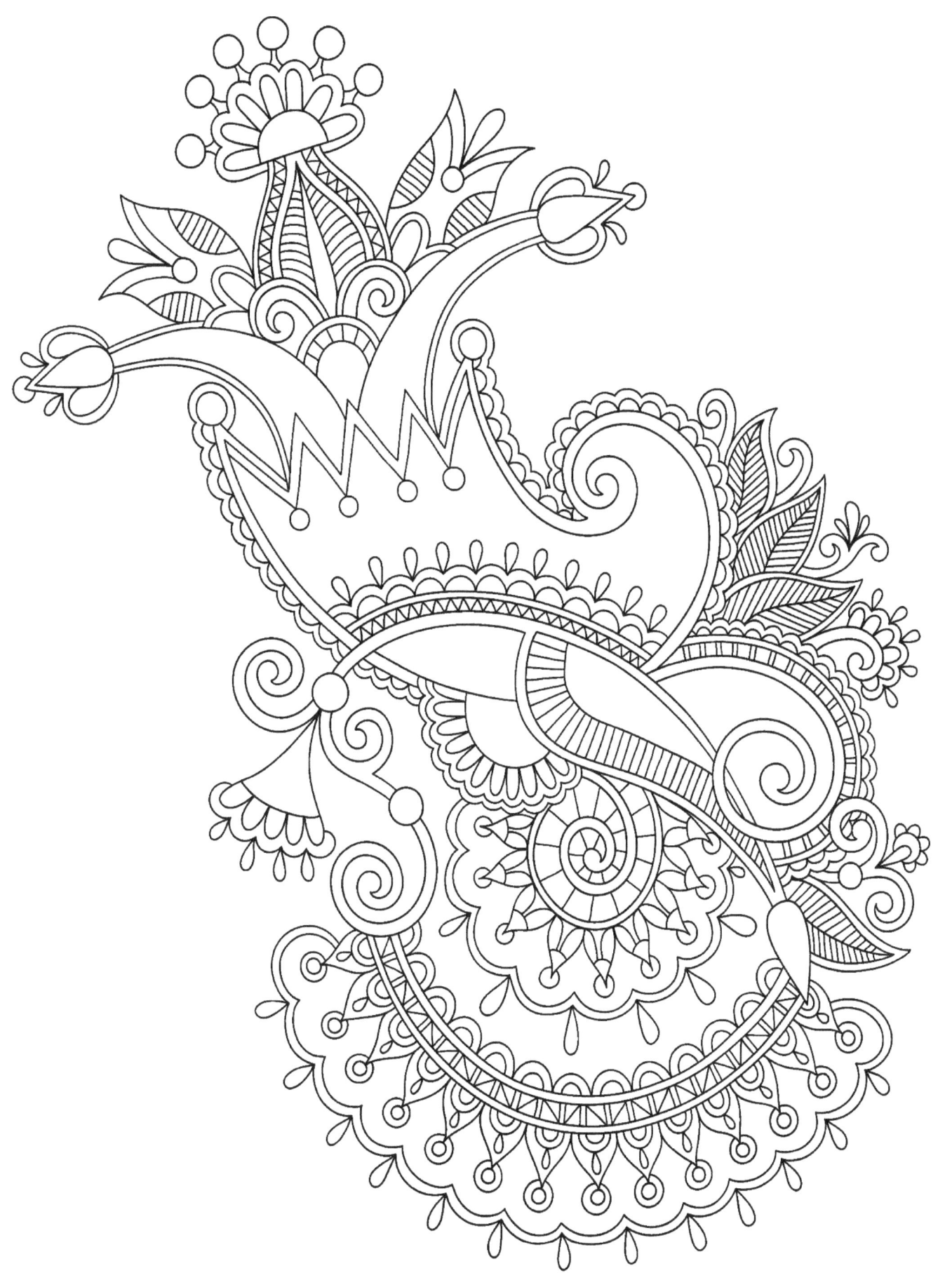

Insert Wax Paper Here

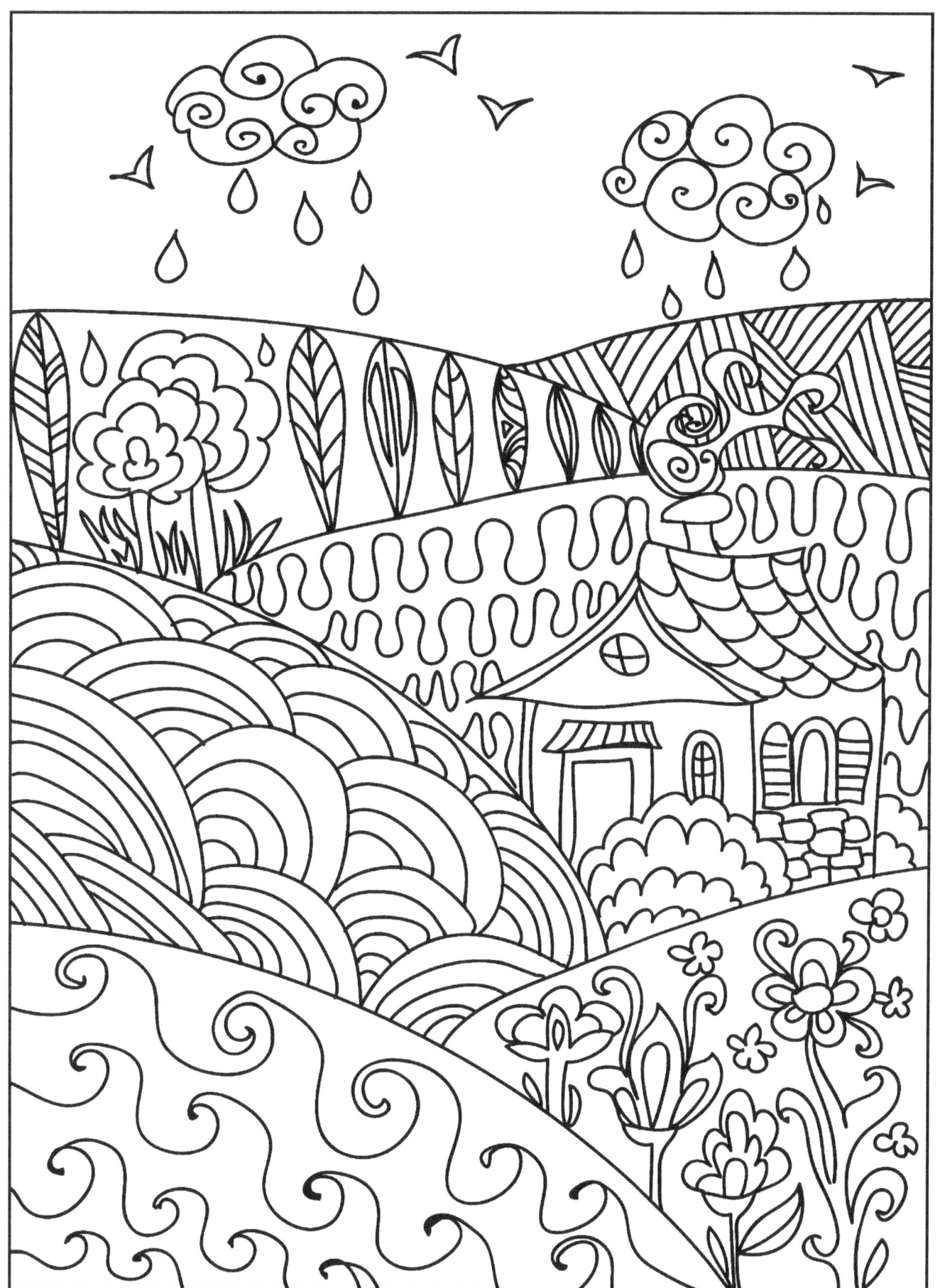

Insert Wax Paper Here

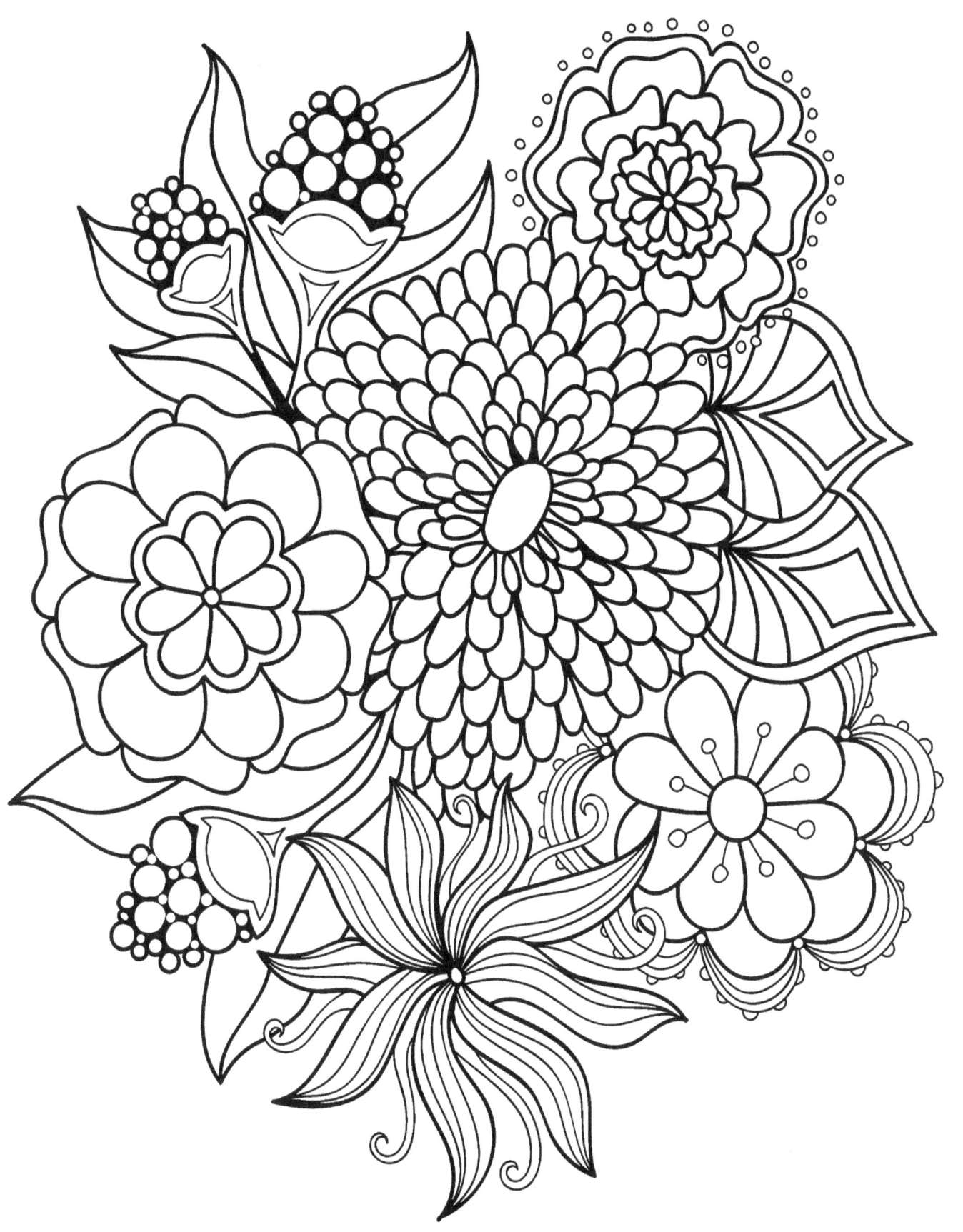

Insert Wax Paper Here

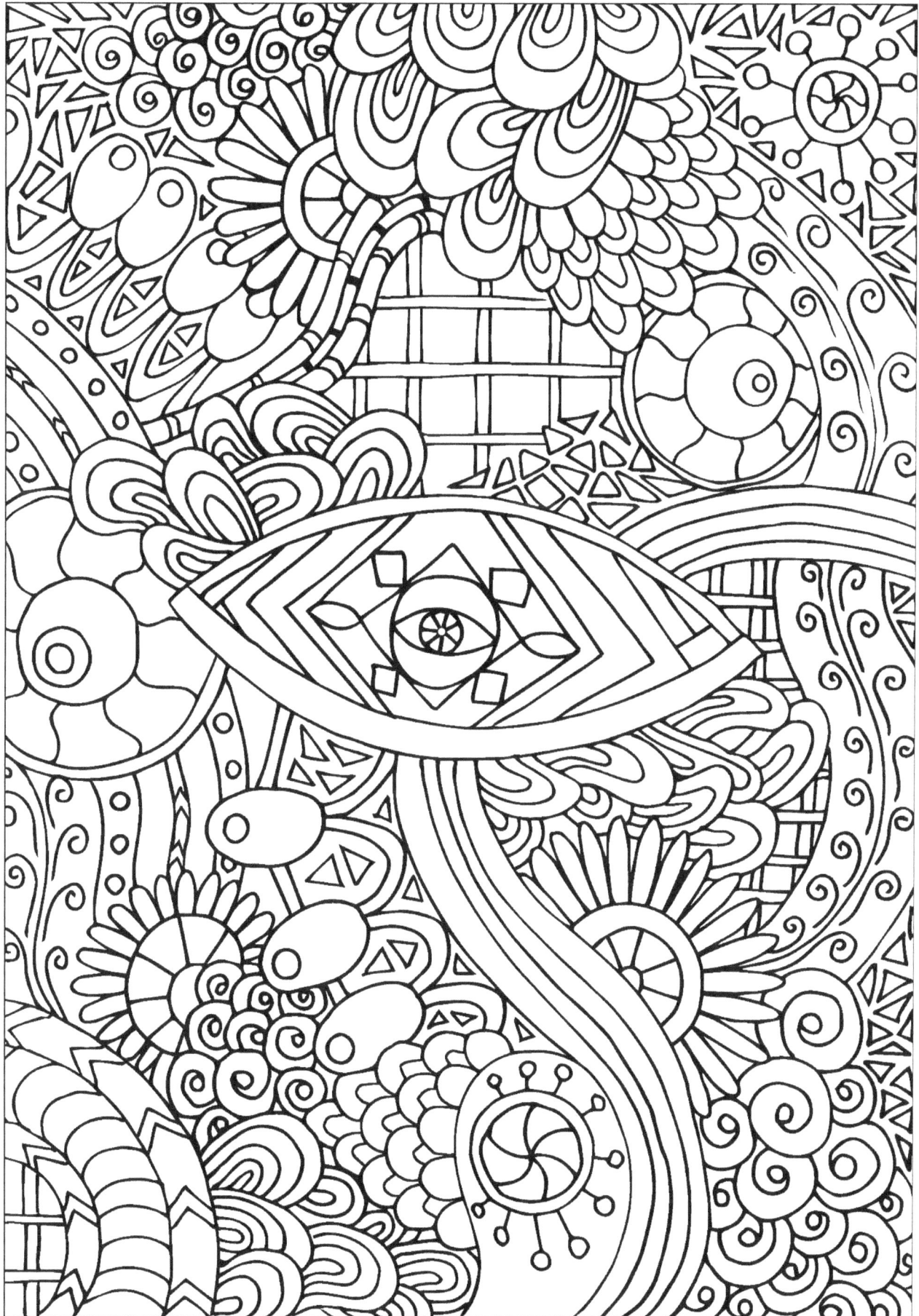

Insert Wax Paper Here

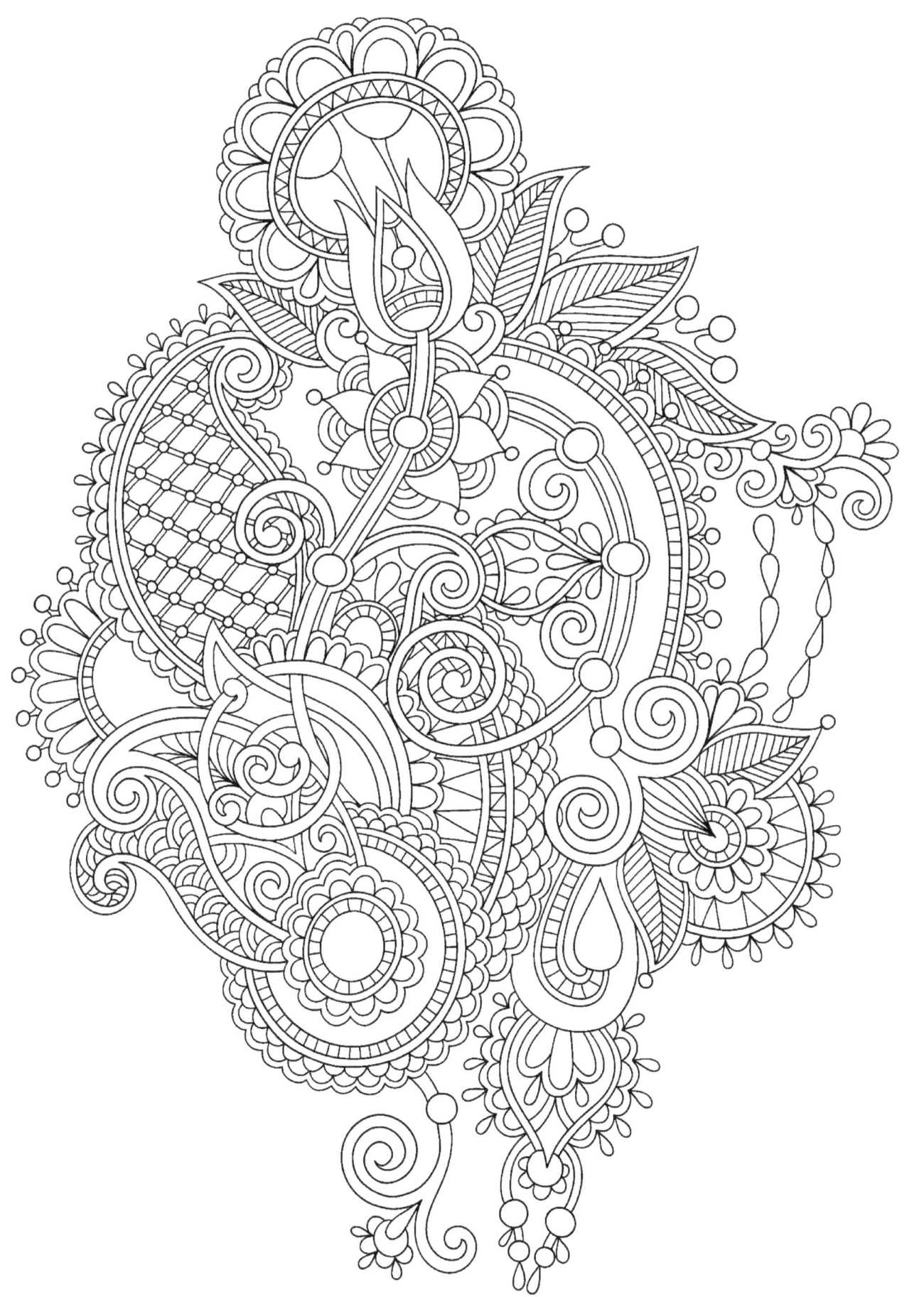

Insert Wax Paper Here

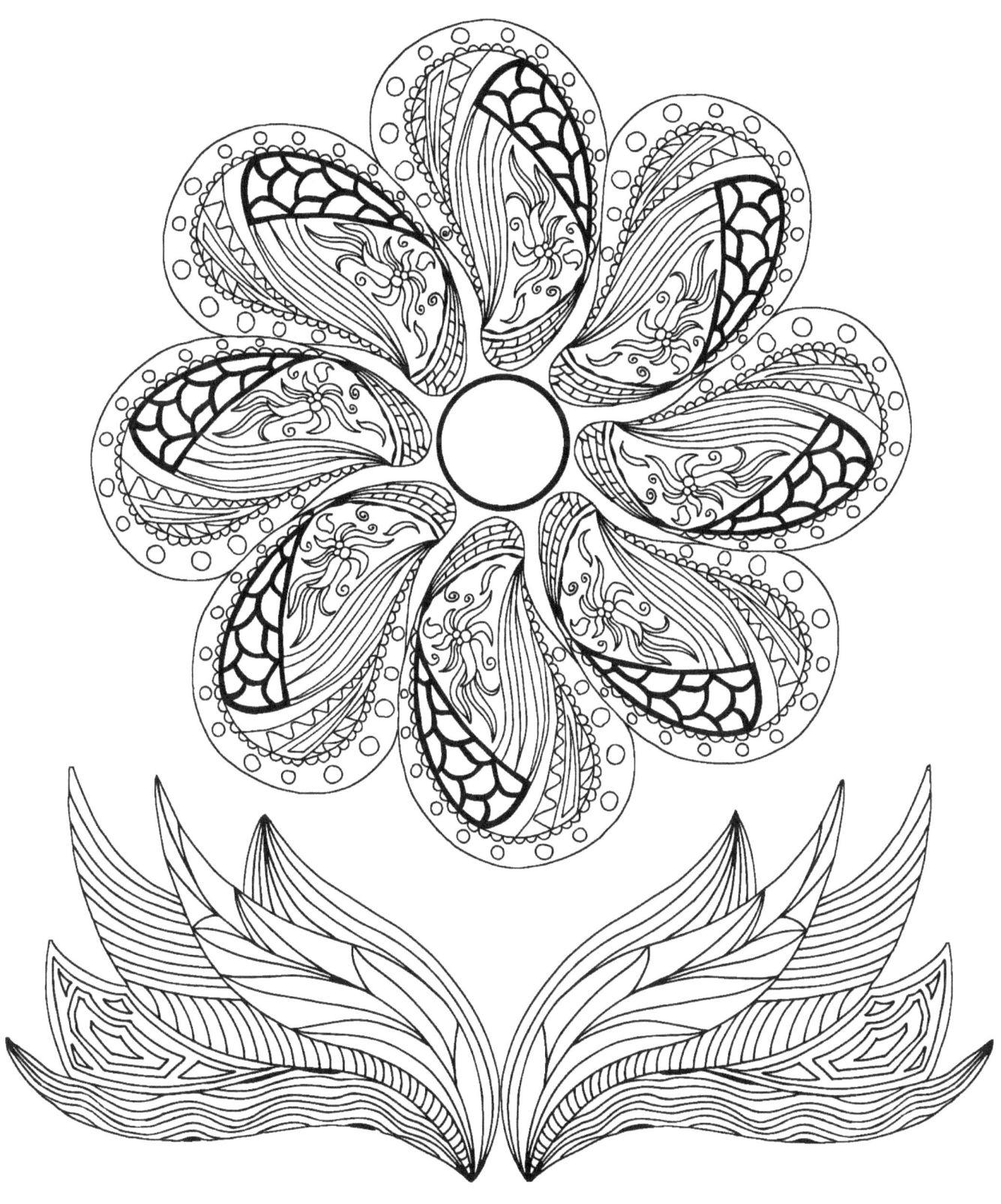

Insert Wax Paper Here

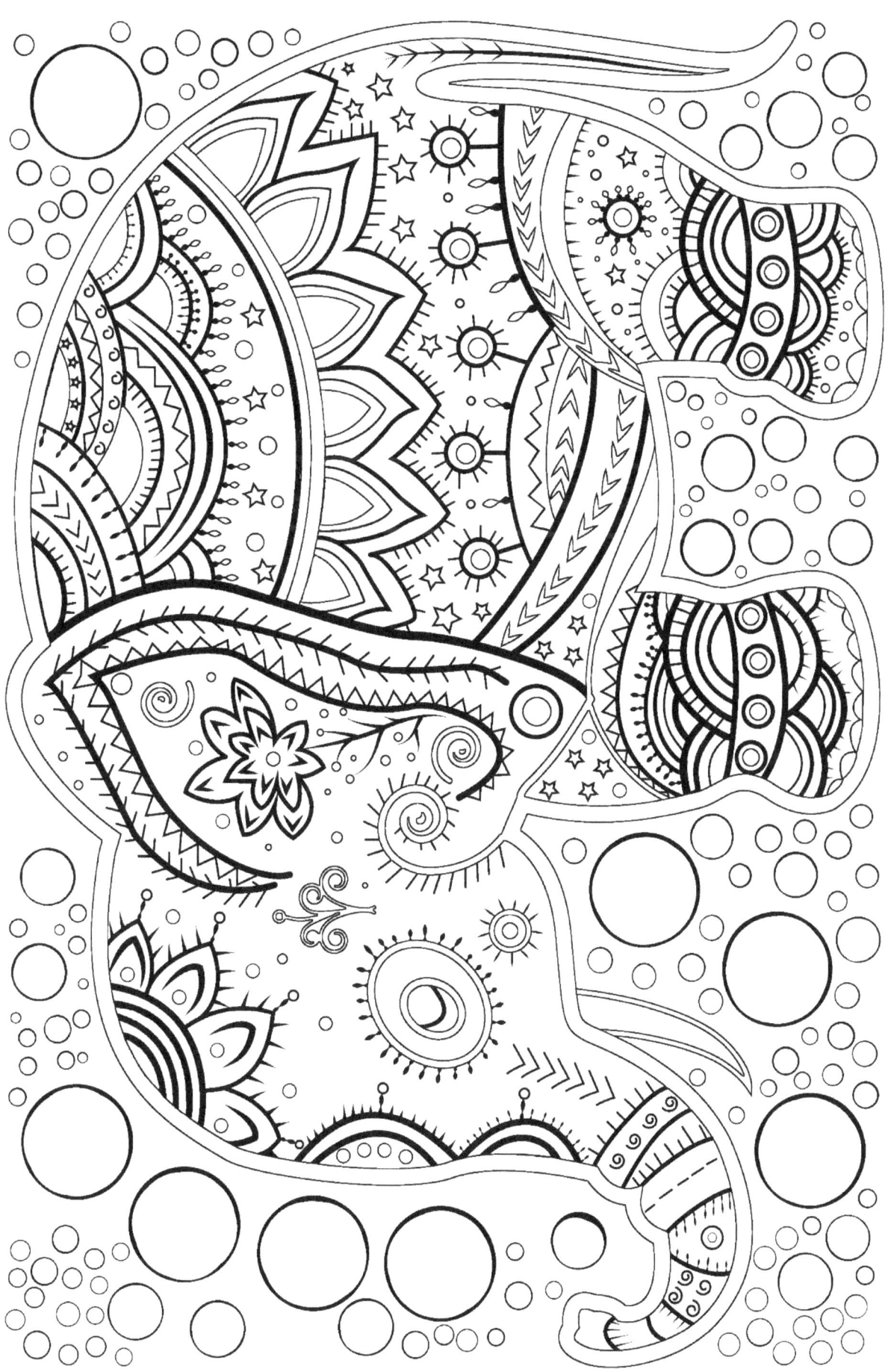

Insert Wax Paper Here

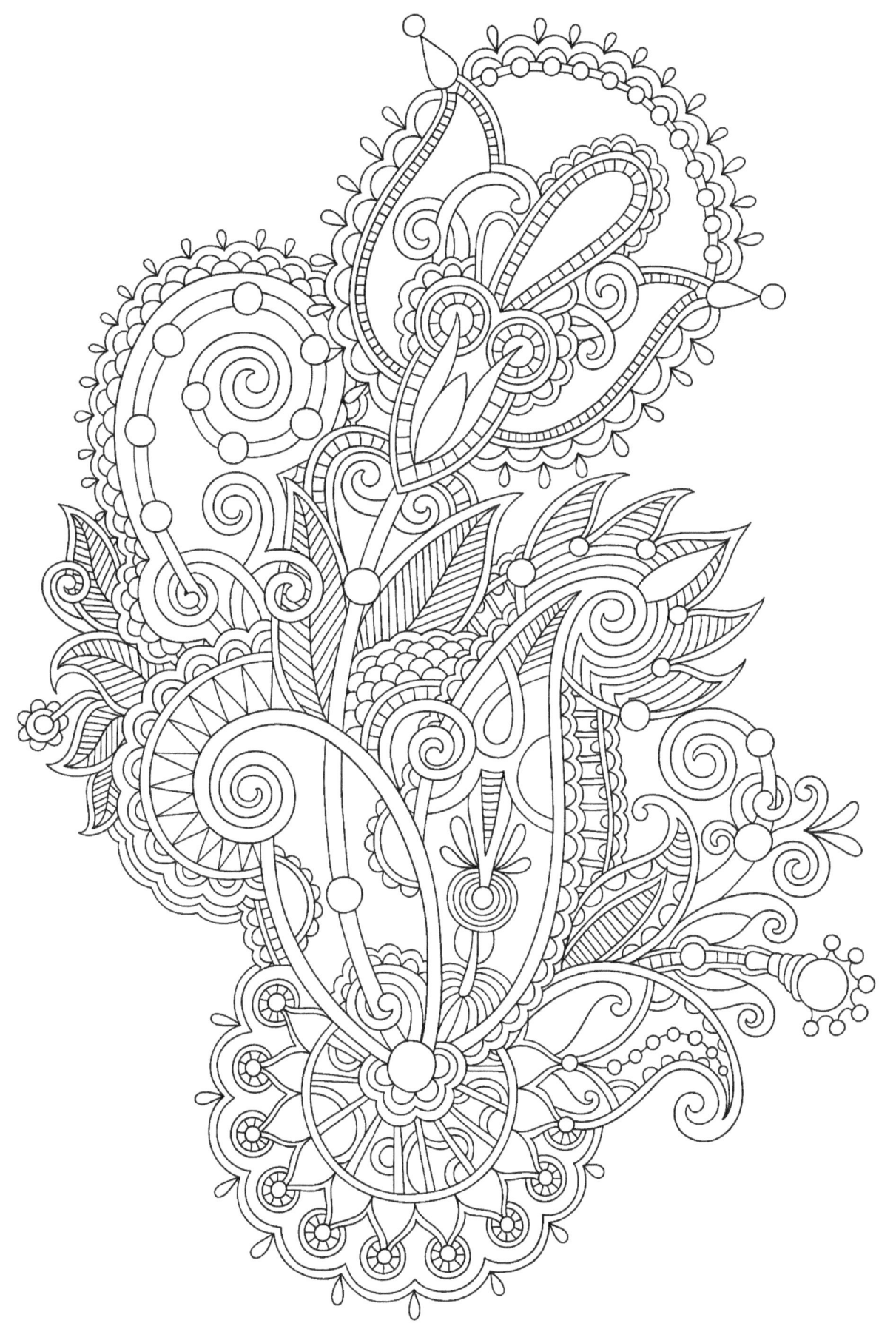

Insert Wax Paper Here

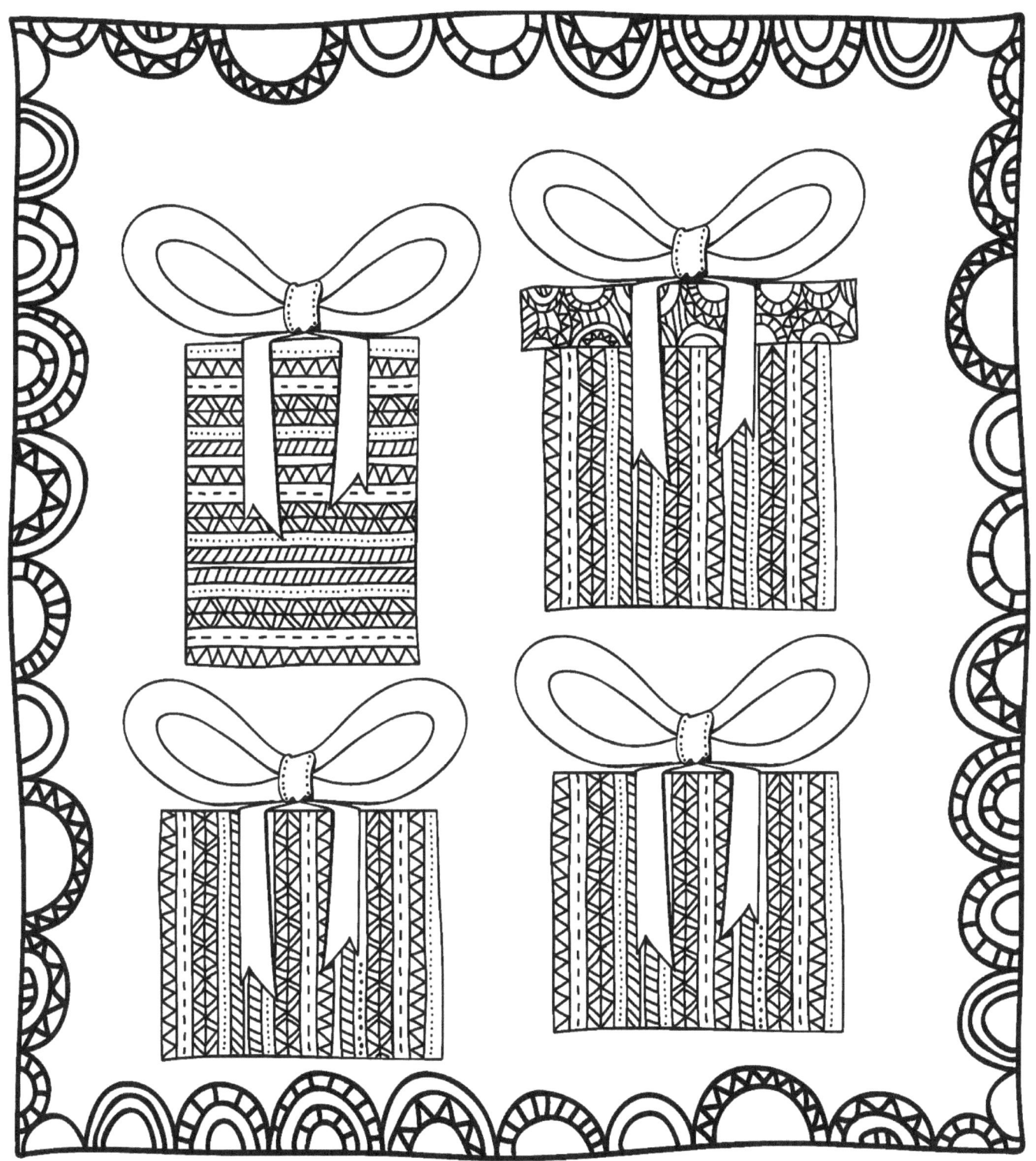

Insert Wax Paper Here

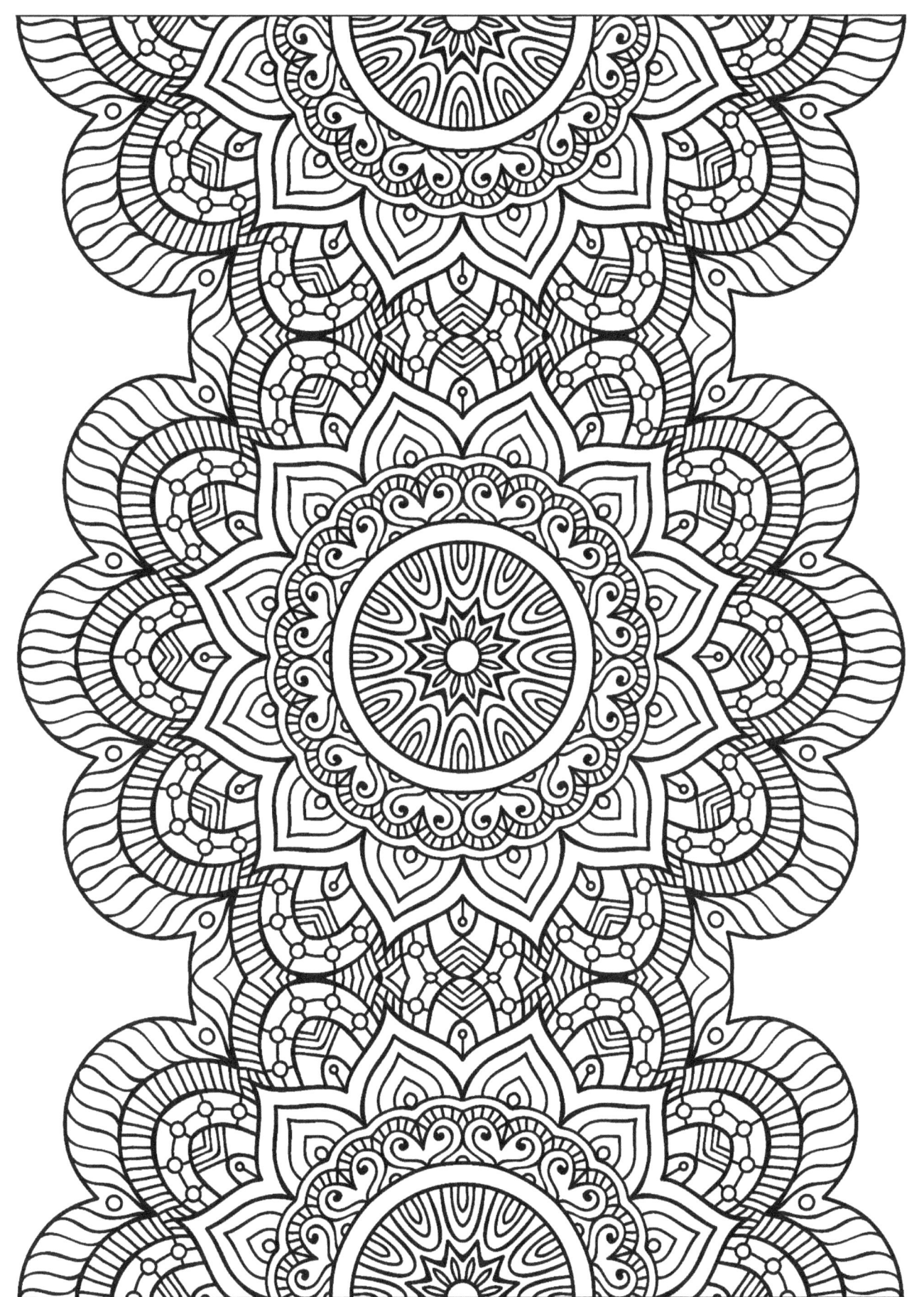

Insert Wax Paper Here

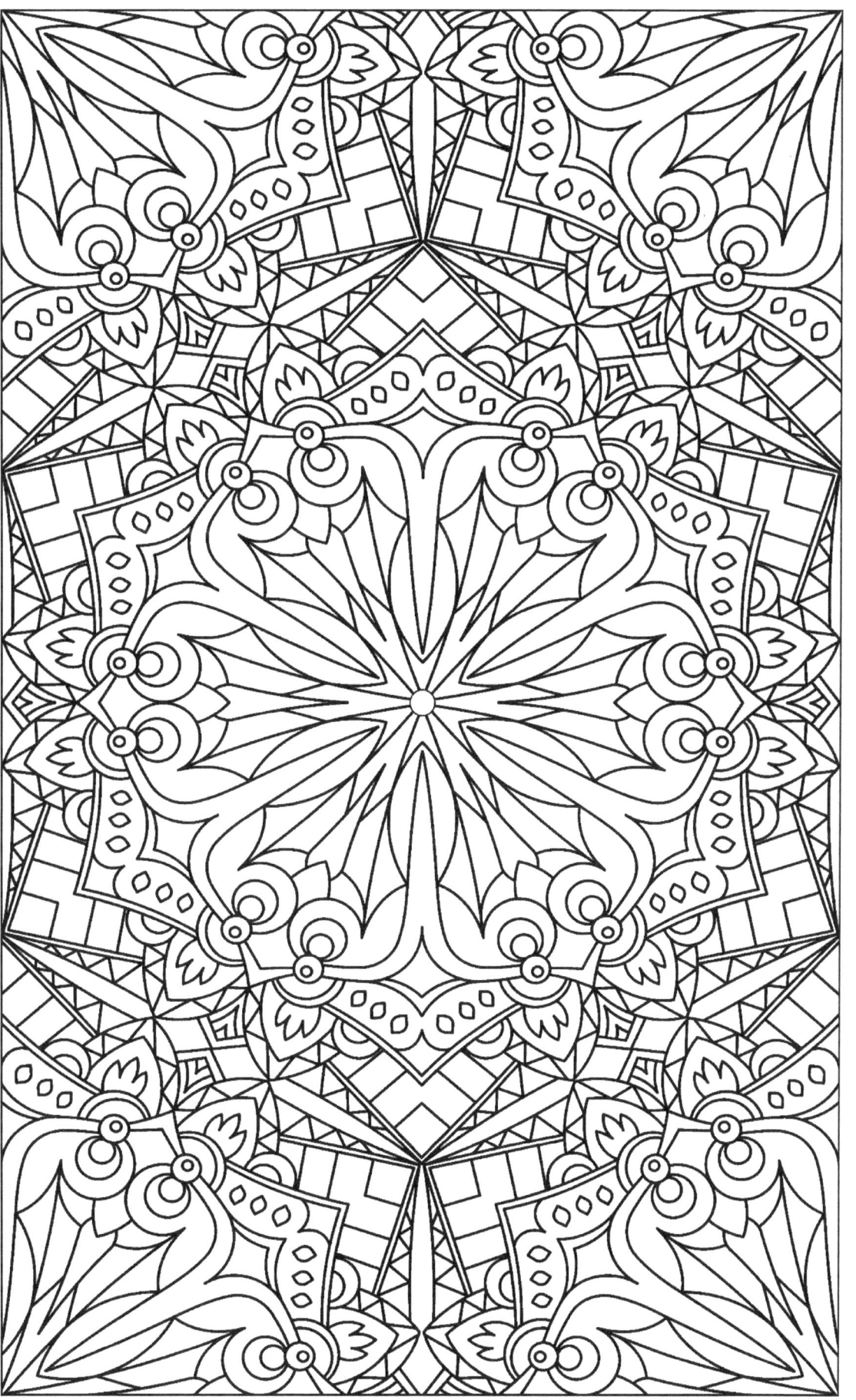

Insert Wax Paper Here

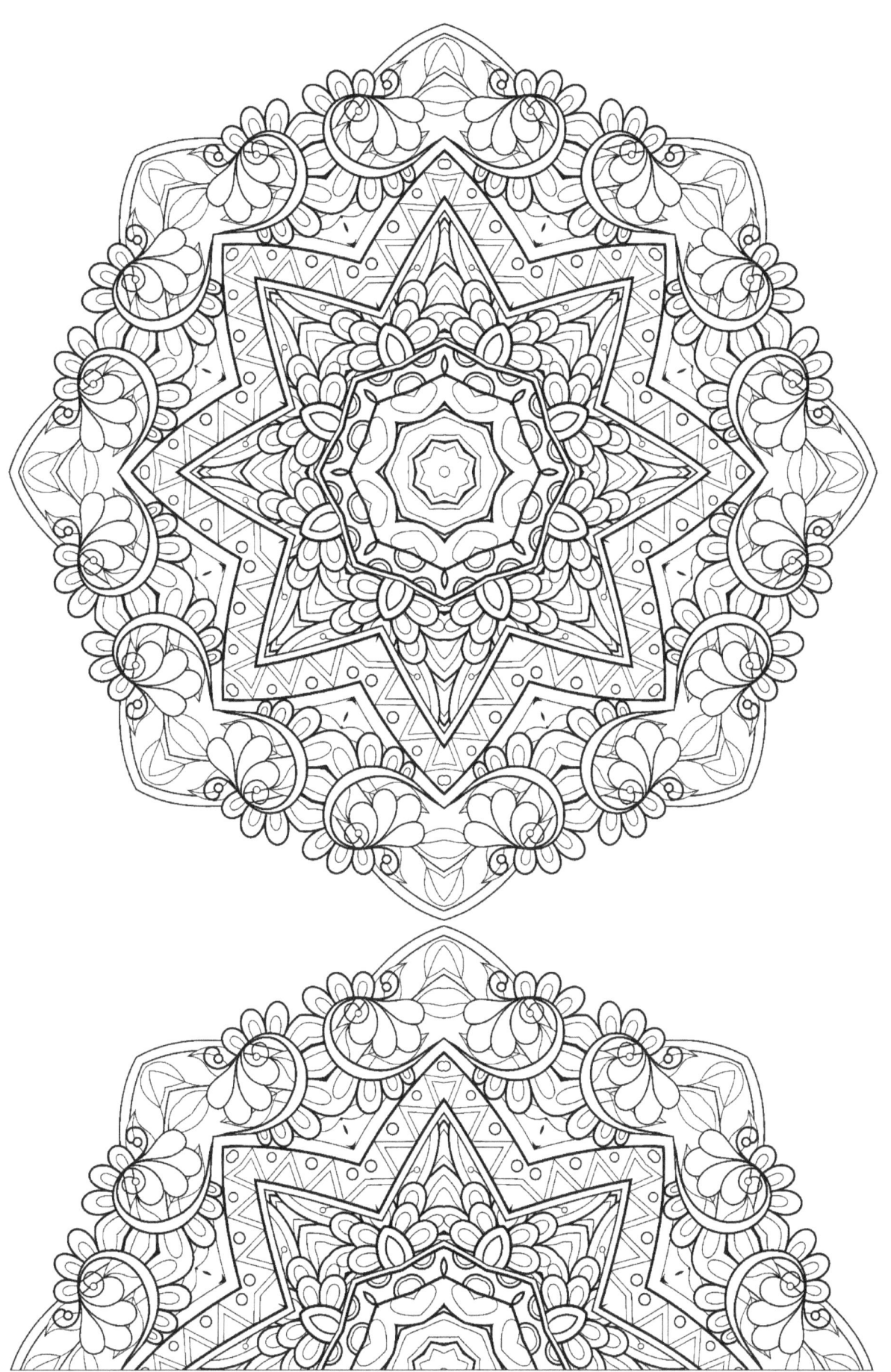

Insert Wax Paper Here

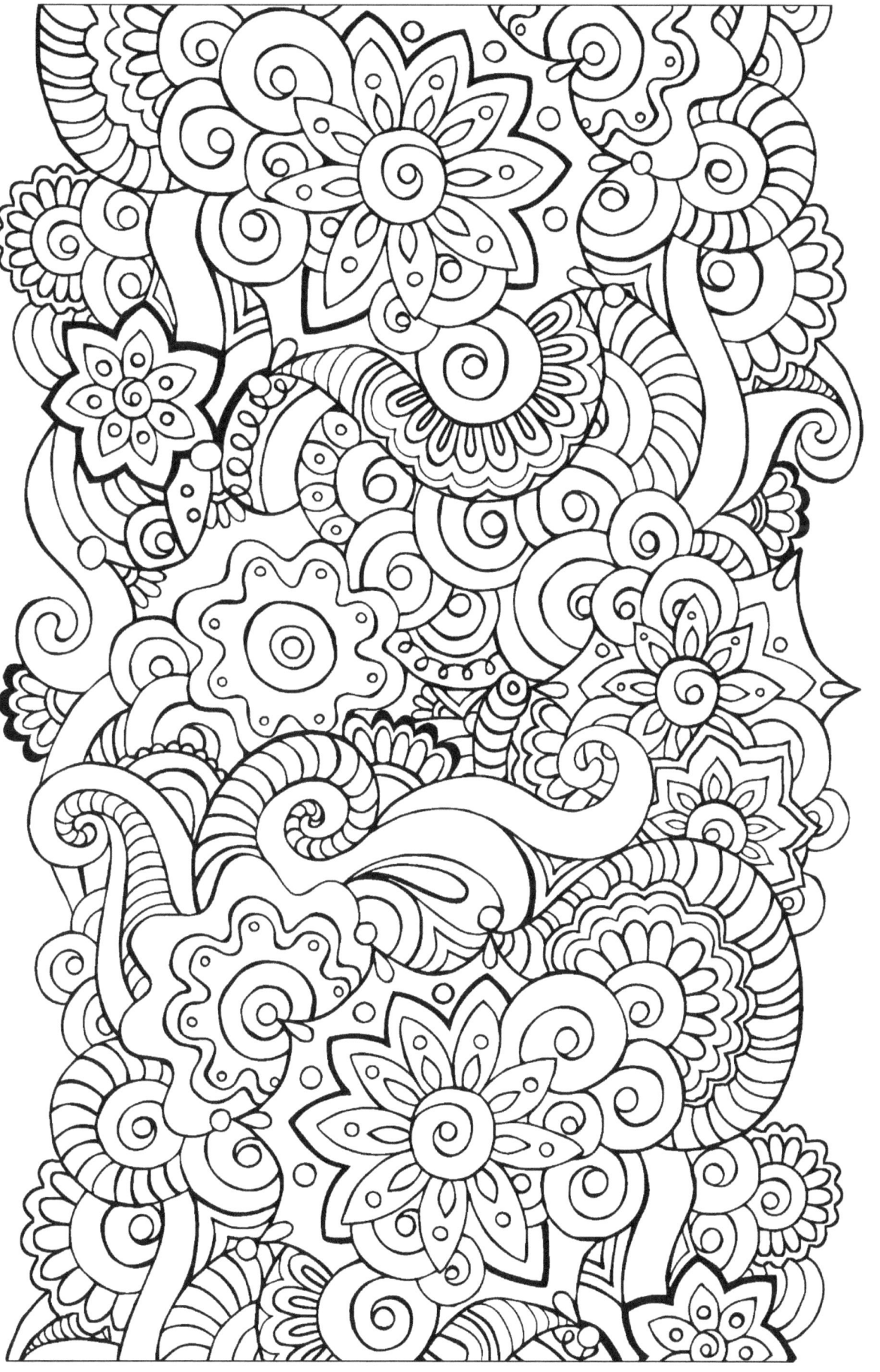

Insert Wax Paper Here

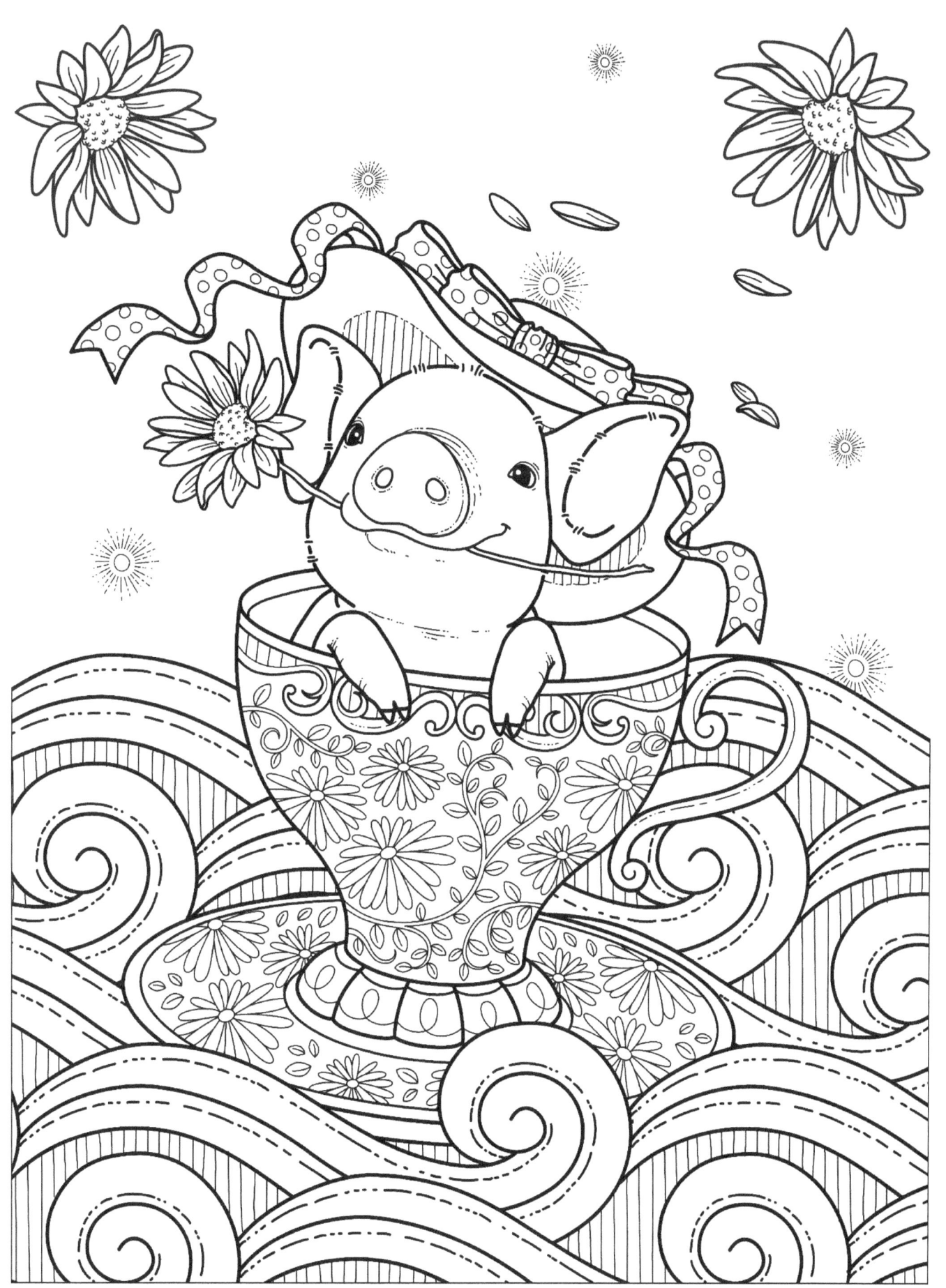

Insert Wax Paper Here

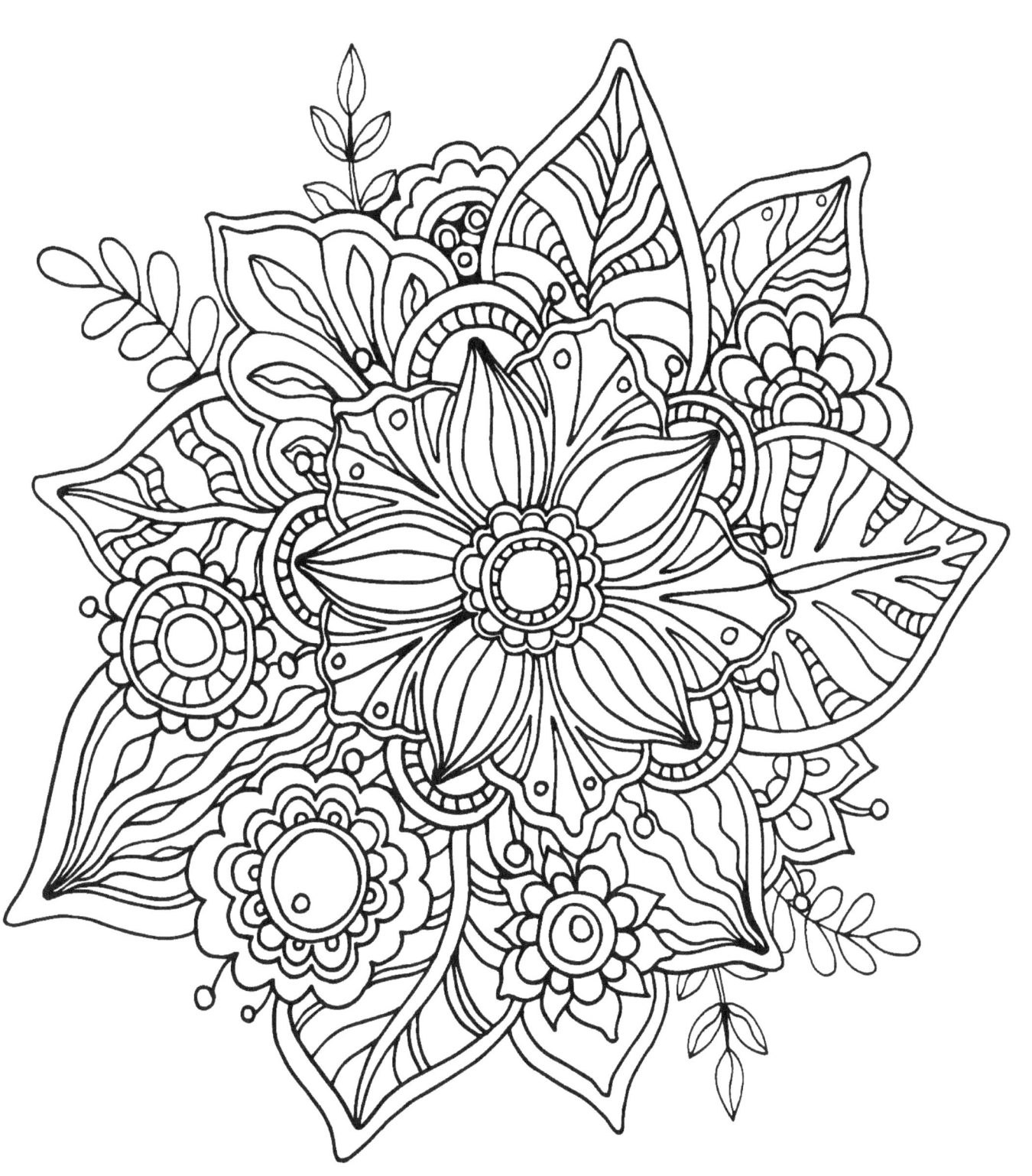

Insert Wax Paper Here

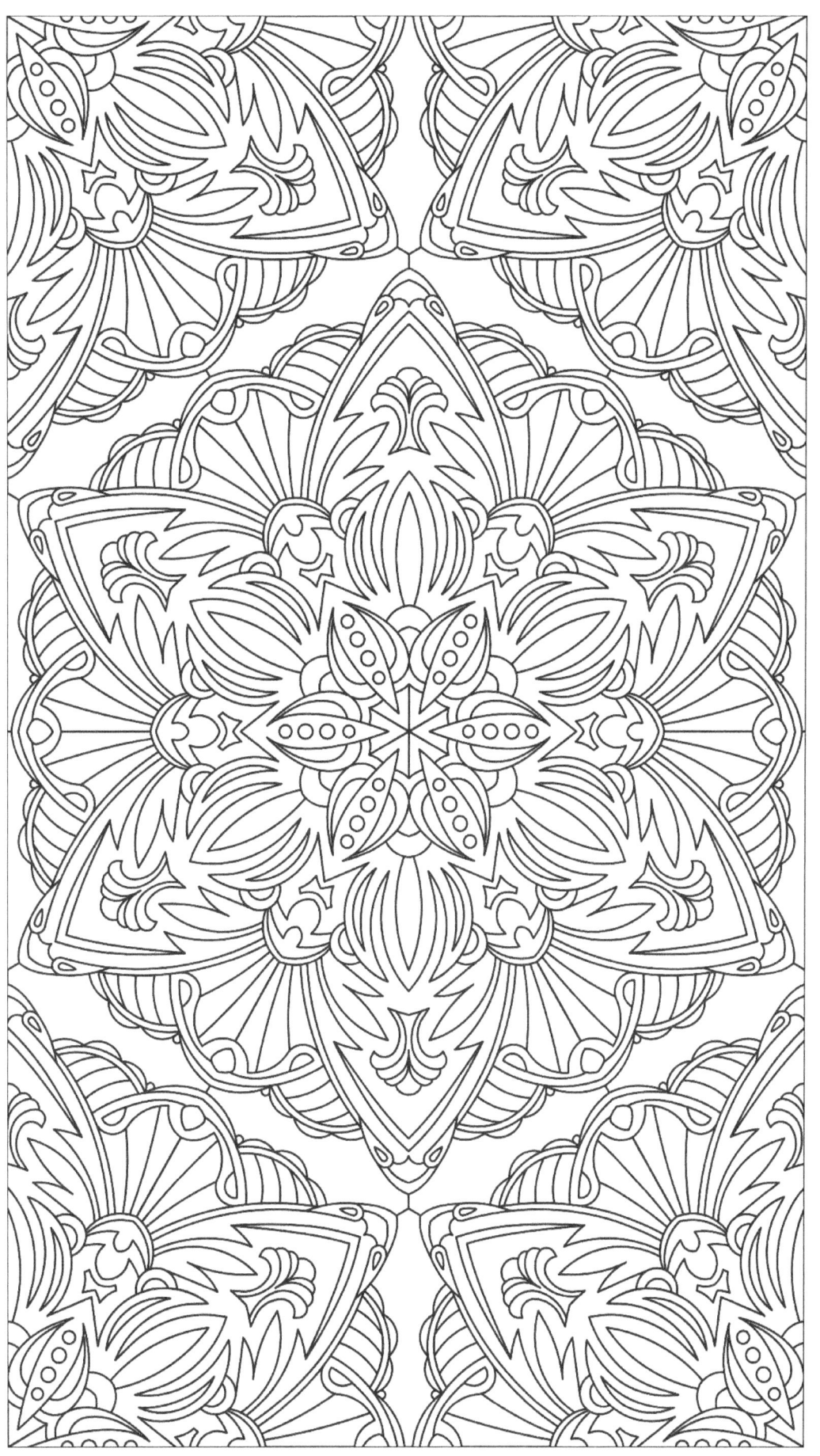

Insert Wax Paper Here

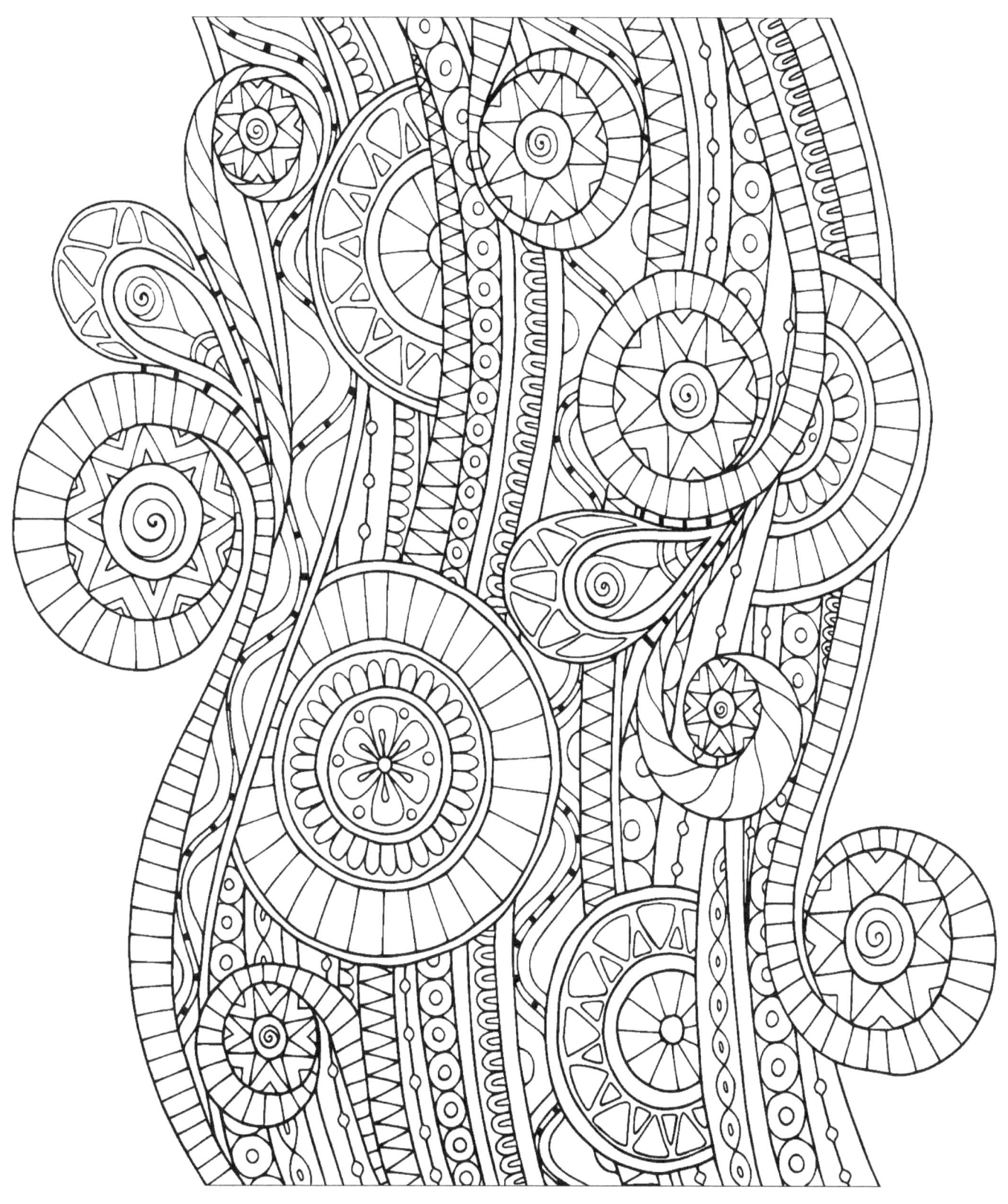

Insert Wax Paper Here

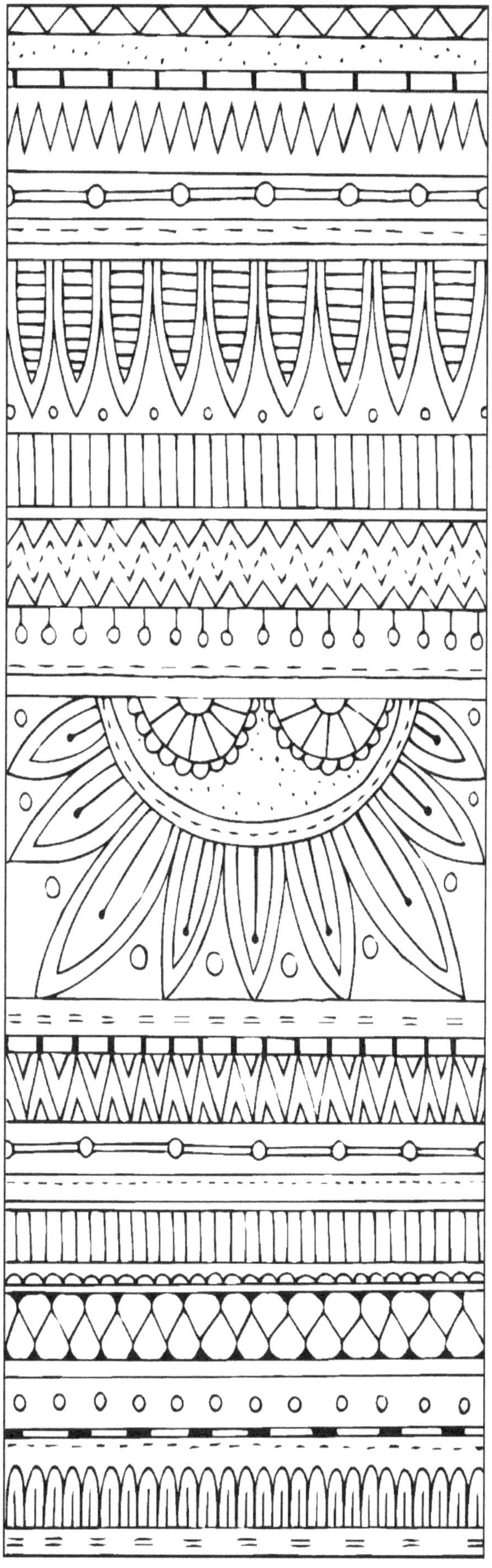
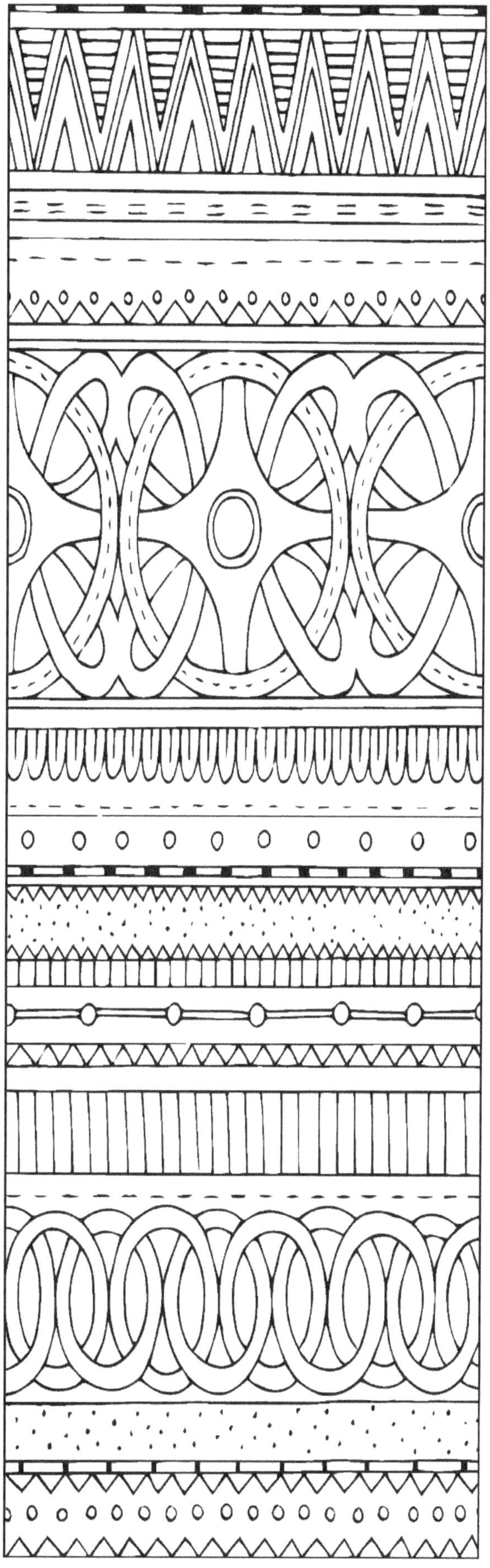

Insert Wax Paper Here

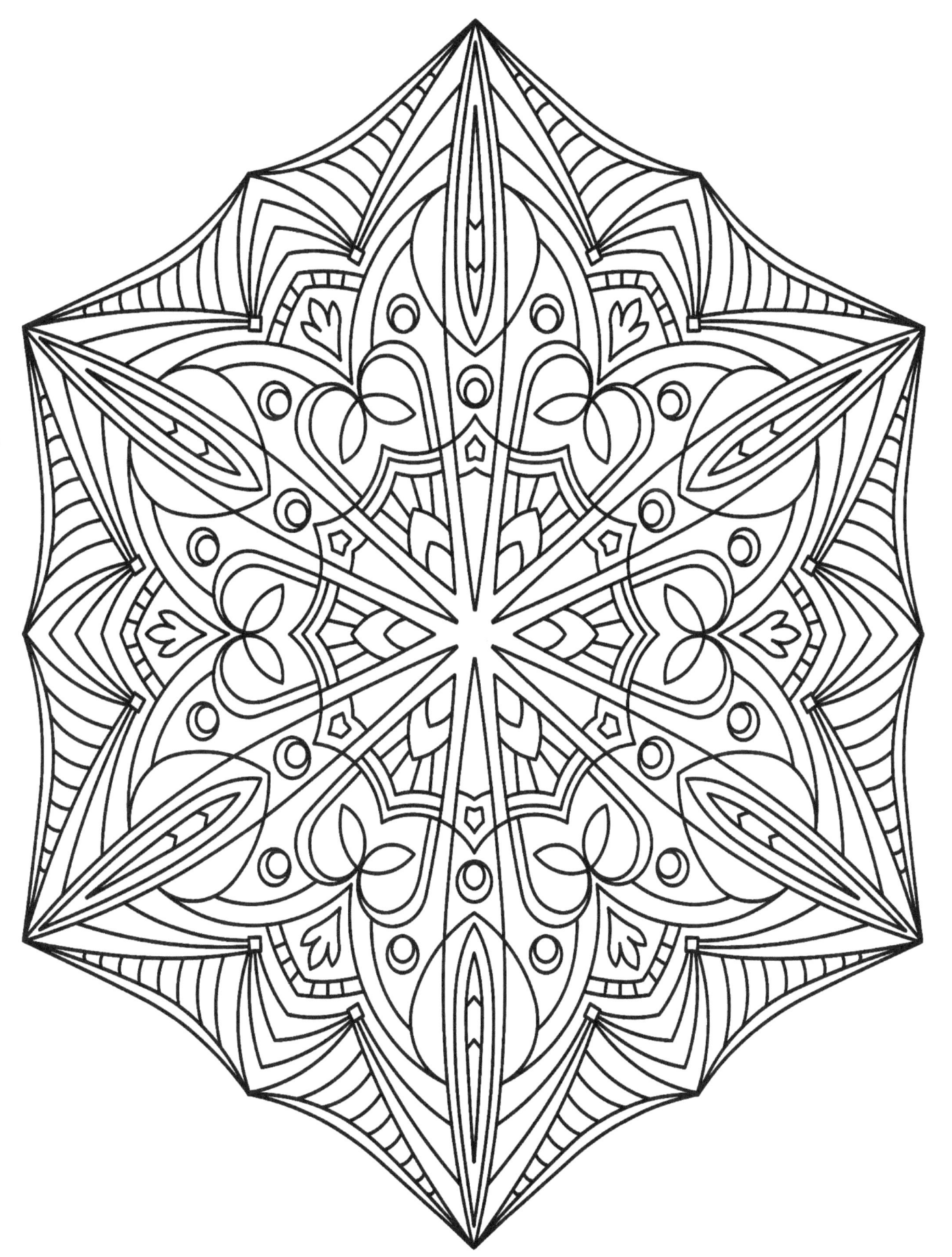

Insert Wax Paper Here

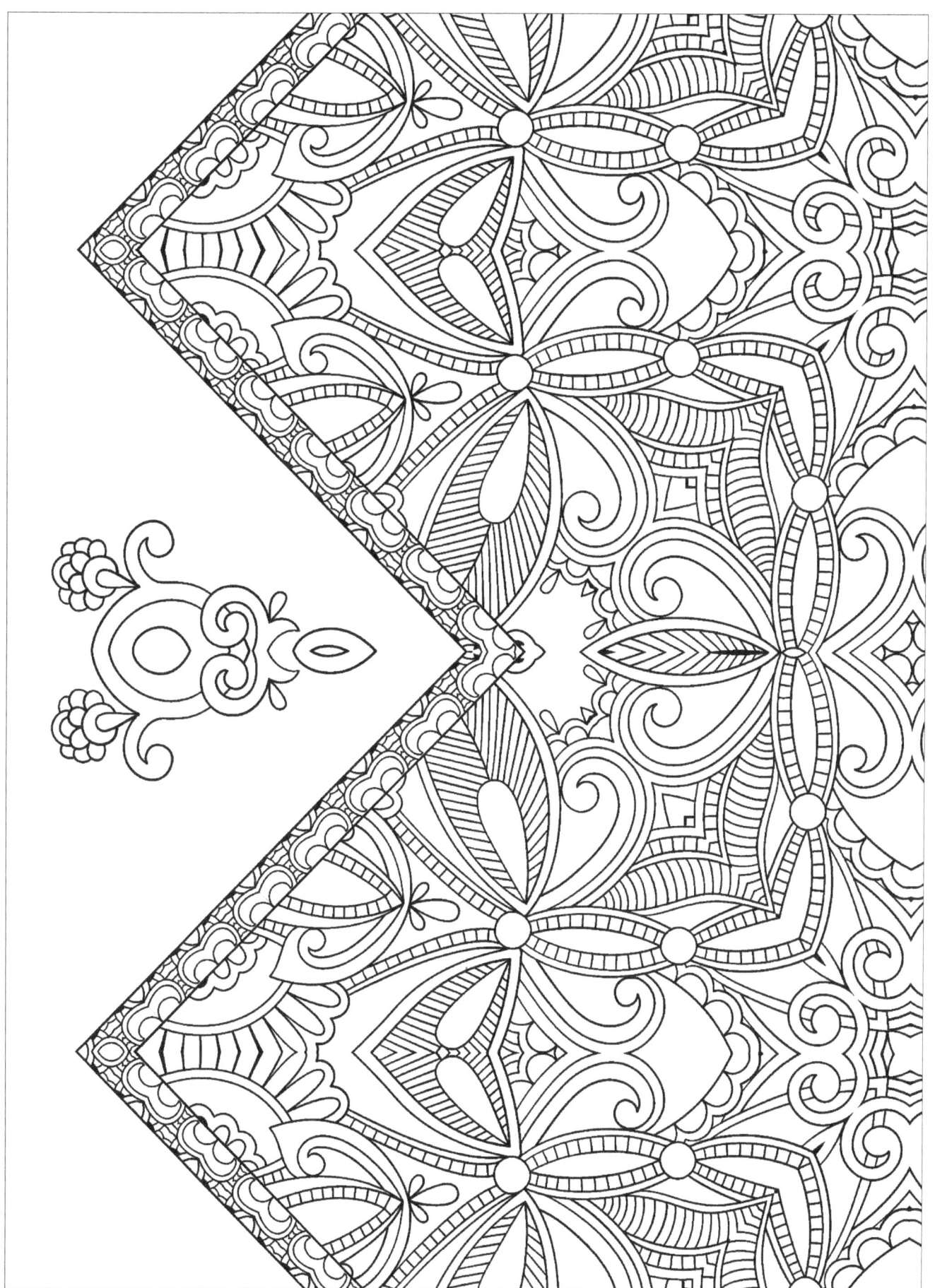

Insert Wax Paper Here

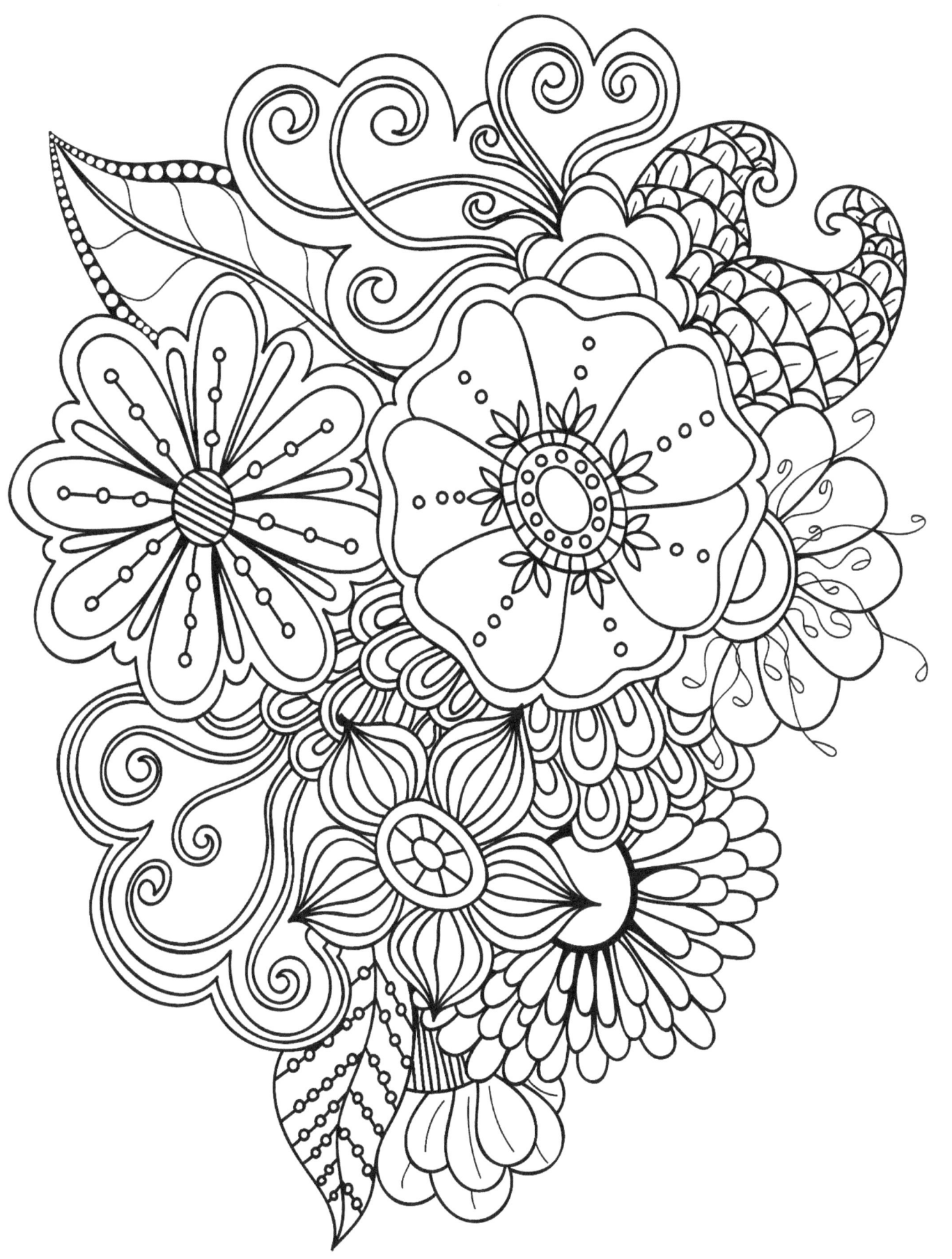